The Ethical Workplace

A Survival Guide for Modern Professionals

Richard Lowe

The Writing King

The Ethical Workplace: A Survival Guide for Modern Professionals

Copyright © 2026 by Richard G Lowe

Table of Contents

Introduction: The Evolving Workplace 6

Chapter 1: What is Ethics? 9

Chapter 2: Why Ethics Matter in the Workplace.................... 13

Chapter 3: Building Effective Teams 17

Chapter 4: Leadership in the Modern Era.............................. 24

Chapter 5: Addressing Problematic Behavior 31

Chapter 6: Communication Excellence 38

Chapter 7: Digital Presence and Social Media 44

Chapter 8: Managing Time and Expectations 51

Chapter 9: Integrity in Action.. 57

Chapter 10: Work-Life Integration 63

Chapter 11: Diversity, Equity, and Inclusion 69

Chapter 12: When DEI Becomes Unethical 76

Chapter 13: Emerging Challenges.. 83

Chapter 14: When the Boss is Not Ethical 90

Chapter 15: When the Company is Not Ethical 97

Chapter 16: Case Study - Enron: When Everything Goes Wrong
.... 104

Chapter 17: Case Study - Theranos: The Charismatic Leader's
Deception 108

Chapter 18: Case Study - Wells Fargo: Pressure, Incentives, and
Individual Choice 112

Chapter 19: Case Study - Cambridge Analytica/Facebook: Data
Ethics in Action 116

Chapter 20: Case Study - Microsoft: Getting Ethics Right.... 121

Chapter 21: Your Responsibility (Yes, Yours)........................126

Conclusion 132

Books by Richard Lowe...137

See books by Richard Lowe at

https://masterofworlds.com

Get free publishing insights and industry updates at

https://thewritingking.substack.com

For ghostwriting and book coaching services see

https://thewritingking.com

Introduction: The Evolving Workplace

Remember when the biggest workplace ethical dilemma was whether it was okay to heat fish in the office microwave? Those were simpler times. Now we're grappling with whether it's ethical to use AI to write our performance reviews, if we should tell our boss that their camera was on during that bathroom break on Zoom, and whether liking your coworker's vacation photos on Instagram counts as stalking.

Welcome to the modern workplace, where ethics have gotten about as complicated as trying to figure out who's on mute during a conference call with twelve people. The rules we learned in 2016 (heck, even the rules we learned in 2020) are evolving faster than the platforms we use to discuss them. Clear-cut guidelines for professional behavior now require the wisdom of Solomon and the patience of a customer service representative dealing with someone who insists they "didn't get the email" that's sitting right there in their inbox.

When I first wrote this book, remote work was something freelancers did, Slack was just getting started, and having work-life balance while your bedroom doubled as your conference room was pure science fiction. Nobody was worried about whether their Ring doorbell would accidentally broadcast their Amazon delivery to the entire sales team, or if using ChatGPT to help write emails was cheating on your job.

Here's the thing about ethics: the core principles haven't changed, even if the situations where we apply them have gotten weirder than a virtual reality team-building exercise. Honesty is still honesty, whether you're telling the truth face-to-face or through a cartoon avatar in a metaverse meeting. Respect is still respect, whether you're showing it in person or by remembering to mute yourself when your dog decides to provide commentary during the quarterly review.

The workplace has transformed so dramatically that we're all pioneers in this brave new world of professional conduct. We're making up the rules as we go along, like early internet users trying to figure out email etiquette. Remember when people used to write emails in ALL CAPS because nobody told them it was shouting? We're in that phase again, except now it's with everything from appropriate Zoom backgrounds to whether the company Slack channel should have a politics section.

This isn't about avoiding HR complaints or staying out of legal trouble, though those are nice side benefits. This is about figuring out how to be a decent human being in a work environment that would have seemed like pure fantasy to our predecessors. How do you build trust with colleagues you've never met in person? How do you maintain integrity when half your work is done by algorithms? How do you show leadership when everyone's a little square on a screen?

Here's the beautiful irony: as technology has made work more complex, it's also made ethics more crucial. When you can work from anywhere, at any time, with anyone in the world, the only thing holding the whole system together is trust. When your boss can't physically see what you're doing, integrity becomes your most valuable currency. When miscommunication can happen faster than you can say "you're on mute," clear, honest communication becomes essential.

So here we are, trying to navigate this new world with the ethical equivalent of assembly instructions where half the diagrams are missing. Some of the old landmarks are still there (treat people with respect, be honest, do good work) but the terrain has changed completely. We've got new obstacles to navigate: the ethics of surveillance software that tracks your keystrokes, the question of whether it's okay to pretend your internet is cutting out when you want to escape a pointless meeting.

This book isn't going to give you a perfect blueprint, because frankly, nobody has one. What it will do is help you think through these new challenges with some humor, common sense, and the recognition that we're all figuring this out together. The cases and principles examined here point toward a consistent framework: ethical workplaces require clarity about what's expected, systems that reward ethical behavior and actually punish unethical behavior, and leaders who model the standards they demand from others. Everything else — the technology, the remote work arrangements, the DEI debates — is really just variations on those three problems. Whether you're a seasoned professional trying to adapt to remote work or a recent graduate who thinks offices are places where older people go to use printers, we're all students in this new classroom of workplace ethics.

The goal isn't to become some kind of ethical superhero who never puts a foot wrong. The goal is to be thoughtful about the choices we make, honest about the challenges we face, and decent to the people we work with (whether they're sitting next to us or on the other side of the planet, whether we're collaborating in person or through whatever new app someone in IT decided we all need to learn this week).

Because at the end of the day, that's what ethics really is: trying to be a good person, even when nobody's watching, even when the technology is confusing, and even when your cat decides to join your video call and somehow becomes the most professional participant in the entire meeting.

Chapter 1: What is Ethics?

Ethics is basically the difference between being the person everyone wants to work with and being the person everyone tries to avoid in the break room. If you've ever wondered why some colleagues seem to effortlessly earn trust while others can't get anyone to believe them about the weather, you're looking at ethics in action.

At its core, ethics is about making good choices when nobody's forcing you to. It's the voice in your head that says "maybe I shouldn't take credit for this idea" or "perhaps I should mention that the client said no before I got them to say yes." Ethics is what separates humans from algorithms (at least for now) and good employees from the ones who make everyone else update their resumes.

Think of ethics as your internal compass for navigating tricky situations. It doesn't always point you toward the easiest path, but it usually keeps you from driving off a cliff. And when you ignore it, it keeps nagging you until you course correct.

The tricky part is that ethics isn't a rulebook you can memorize, like learning that you shouldn't microwave fish in the office kitchen or that replying all to company-wide emails about the broken printer makes you a monster. Ethics is more like jazz improvisation: you need to know the basic principles, but then you have to figure out how to apply them to whatever weird situation you find yourself in.

Let's start with the foundation. Most ethical frameworks boil down to a few basic questions: Does this hurt someone? Is this fair? Would I want everyone to act this way? Am I being honest? These might sound simple, but try applying them to modern workplace scenarios and you'll quickly realize why philosophy professors have job security.

Take the classic question of whether you should tell your boss that their presentation has a typo on every slide. The utilitarian approach says you should speak up because the greatest good for the greatest number of people includes saving your boss from public embarrassment. The duty-based approach says you have an obligation to be honest regardless of the consequences. The virtue ethics approach asks what a courageous and kind person would do. Your gut says you should probably mention it but maybe not right before they go on stage.

Personal values make this even more complicated. Your upbringing, culture, religion, and that one really influential teacher you had in college all contribute to your ethical framework. Some people were raised to believe that loyalty is the highest virtue, so they'll never criticize their team even when the team is clearly wrong. Others were taught that honesty trumps everything else, so they'll point out problems even when it makes everyone uncomfortable.

The workplace adds another layer of complexity because you're not just dealing with your own values. You're working with people who might have completely different ethical frameworks. Your colleague who grew up in a culture that values harmony might never directly disagree with anyone, while your other colleague who was raised to "speak truth to power" might challenge every decision. Neither approach is wrong, but they can create interesting dynamics in team meetings.

Cultural considerations are huge in today's global workplace. What counts as ethical behavior varies dramatically across cultures. Direct eye contact during conversations is seen as respectful honesty in some cultures and aggressive disrespect in others. The concept of time, gift-giving, hierarchy, and even the definition of truth can vary depending on who you're working with.

Religious considerations add another dimension. Some people's ethical frameworks are deeply rooted in religious teachings, while others are completely secular. The key is recognizing that everyone's operating from some kind of moral foundation, even if it's just "try not to be a jerk to people." The goal isn't to convert everyone to your way of thinking but to find common ground that allows everyone to work together ethically.

Here's where it gets really interesting: professional standards often conflict with personal values. Your company might have a policy that technically allows something your personal ethics say is wrong, or vice versa. Maybe your personal values say you should always be completely honest, but your professional environment requires a certain amount of diplomatic filtering. Learning to navigate these conflicts without compromising your core principles is one of the biggest challenges in workplace ethics.

The good news is that most ethical decisions aren't about choosing between good and evil. They're about choosing between different goods or different approaches to solving problems. The challenge is developing the judgment to recognize which situations require careful ethical consideration and which are just normal workplace decisions.

Some people think ethics is about following rules, but rules can't cover every situation. Ethics is about developing good judgment and the courage to act on it. It's about building the habit of pausing to consider the implications of your actions, not just for yourself but for everyone who might be affected.

The goal isn't to become some kind of moral perfectionist who agonizes over every decision. The goal is to become someone who consistently tries to do the right thing, even when it's inconvenient, even when nobody's watching, and even when the right thing isn't immediately obvious.

Because here's the truth about workplace ethics: people notice. They notice when you take credit for someone else's work, when you throw colleagues under the bus to save yourself, when you promise things you can't deliver, and when you pretend problems don't exist. They also notice when you give credit where it's due, when you take responsibility for mistakes, when you keep your word, and when you address problems honestly.

Your reputation for ethical behavior becomes one of your most valuable professional assets. It determines who trusts you with important projects, who wants to work with you on teams, who refers opportunities to you, and who vouches for you when you're not in the room. In a world where your LinkedIn profile can follow you for your entire career, your ethical reputation is worth protecting.

The reason your ethical reputation matters so much is that it travels ahead of you. People form opinions before they meet you, and those opinions are built from the accumulation of small choices you made when you thought nobody was paying attention. Most of them were. And yes, including the lunch from the refrigerator.

Chapter 2: Why Ethics Matter in the Workplace

You might be thinking, "Great, another lecture about why I should be a good person at work. What's next, a reminder to chew with my mouth closed during lunch meetings?" But stick with me here, because the business case for ethics is way more compelling than you might expect, and frankly, way more selfish than most ethics books will admit.

Trust is the currency that keeps everything running. When people trust you, projects move faster, decisions get made easier, and everyone stops double-checking your work like you're an intern who might accidentally delete the entire customer database. Trust means your boss doesn't feel the need to micromanage you, your colleagues don't feel like they need to cover their backs when working with you, and clients don't require seventeen layers of approval before moving forward with your recommendations.

Trust also means you get the benefit of the doubt when things go wrong. And things will go wrong. The server will crash right before the big presentation, the client will change their mind after you've already done the work, or you'll accidentally send an email complaining about someone to that exact someone. When you have a reputation for ethical behavior, people assume these mistakes are just bad luck. When you don't have that reputation, people assume you're incompetent or malicious.

Here's what most people don't realize: ethical behavior is practical. It eliminates so many potential problems that it's basically like having a superpower. When you consistently tell the truth, you never have to remember what lies you told to whom. When you give credit where it's due, you don't have to worry about someone exposing you as a fraud. When you treat people fairly, you don't have to watch your back for revenge plots.

Think about the mental energy it takes to maintain unethical behavior. You have to keep track of who knows what, who you've promised different things to, and who might blow up your carefully constructed house of cards. People who cut ethical corners spend an enormous amount of time and energy managing the fallout from their shortcuts. People who behave ethically get to use that same energy for productive work.

The legal versus ethical distinction is crucial here, and not just because legal problems can ruin your career. Legal is the bare minimum, the floor below which you absolutely cannot go without facing serious consequences. Ethical is the standard that makes people want to work with you. You can be completely legal and still be the kind of person everyone avoids at company parties.

Legal says you can't discriminate based on protected classes. Ethical says you should try to be inclusive and fair to everyone. Legal says you can't steal company property. Ethical says you shouldn't take credit for other people's ideas or use company resources for personal projects. Legal says you can't lie to investigators. Ethical says you should be honest in your day-to-day interactions, even when nobody's checking up on you.

The consequences of ethical and unethical choices compound in ways that can surprise you. That small lie you told to cover up a minor mistake might seem harmless, but it establishes a pattern. The next time you're tempted to lie, it's easier because you've already crossed that line. Before you know it, you're the person nobody trusts with important information because everyone knows you'll massage the truth when it's convenient.

Small ethical choices build momentum too. When you admit a mistake early and propose a solution, people learn they can count on you to handle problems responsibly. When you give honest feedback even when it's uncomfortable, people learn they can trust your judgment. When you keep confidences and honor your commitments, people learn they can rely on you.

An ethical reputation becomes self-reinforcing. People start bringing you into important conversations because they know you won't leak information inappropriately. They trust you with bigger projects because they know you'll be honest about problems before they become disasters. They recommend you for promotions because they know you'll handle increased responsibility well.

The business world is smaller than you think, especially within industries. The colleague you treat poorly today might be your boss tomorrow. The client you mislead might end up at your next company. The competitor you badmouth might become your acquisition target. Ethical behavior isn't just about being a good person; it's about building relationships that will serve you throughout your career.

Here's something nobody talks about: unethical behavior is exhausting. It requires constant vigilance, creative storytelling, and an impressive memory for all the various versions of truth you've told different people. Ethical behavior is relaxing. You can tell the same story to everyone because it's true. You can sleep well knowing you haven't screwed anyone over. You can focus on doing good work instead of managing the consequences of bad behavior.

The connection between ethics and performance is stronger than most people realize. Teams with high ethical standards communicate better because everyone feels safe being honest about problems. Projects run smoother because nobody's hiding mistakes or covering up issues. Innovation happens faster because people are willing to share ideas without worrying about getting their credit stolen.

Companies with strong ethical cultures attract better talent and keep good people longer. Nobody wants to work in an environment where they have to constantly watch their backs or wonder if their colleagues are undermining them. Ethical workplaces feel safer, more collaborative, and more fun. People do their best work when they trust their teammates and leadership.

The ripple effects extend beyond your immediate team. When customers trust your company, they're more likely to recommend you to others, forgive mistakes, and stick with you during difficult times. When suppliers trust your company, they're more likely to give you favorable terms, prioritize your orders, and work with you to solve problems. When investors trust your company, they're more willing to provide capital and support during challenging periods.

Let's be honest about the real reason ethics matter in the workplace: because unethical behavior will eventually catch up with you, and when it does, the consequences are usually much worse than whatever short-term gain you thought you were getting. The business world is full of cautionary tales about people who thought they were clever enough to cut corners without getting caught.

The irony is that many unethical choices don't even provide significant advantages. The colleague who takes credit for team successes might get a temporary boost, but they also lose the trust and cooperation that could have led to much bigger successes. The manager who lies to cover up departmental problems might avoid short-term criticism, but they also prevent the kind of honest problem-solving that could improve their team's performance.

Ethics matter in the workplace because work is fundamentally a social activity. We're all trying to accomplish things together, and that requires cooperation, communication, and trust. Ethical behavior makes all of these things easier and more effective. Unethical behavior makes everything harder, slower, and more stressful for everyone involved.

The competitive edge is real. In a world where everyone's resume looks more or less the same, being known as someone who can be trusted completely — by colleagues, clients, and managers — is actually rare. That reputation compounds the same way unethical behavior does, just in the other direction.

Chapter 3: Building Effective Teams

Working in teams is a lot like living with roommates, except your roommates can get you fired and you can't solve disputes by eating their leftovers. The good news is that most of the same principles apply: communication, respect, and not leaving messes for other people to clean up. The bad news is that unlike roommates, you can't just move out when things get weird.

The challenge with modern teams is that half the time you're working with people you've never met in person, trying to build relationships through a screen. Video calls help, but there's something fundamentally different about working with someone when you've never shared physical space. You miss all the subtle social cues that help build relationships, and it's easier to forget that your colleagues are humans with lives and feelings outside of their little video squares.

Remote team building requires more intentional effort. You can't rely on casual hallway conversations or impromptu coffee breaks to build relationships. You have to create opportunities for people to connect as humans, not just as job functions. This doesn't mean mandatory virtual happy hours that everyone secretly hates, but it might mean starting meetings with a few minutes of conversation or creating informal channels where people can share non-work updates.

Accountability in distributed teams gets tricky because you can't just walk over to someone's desk and ask how things are going. You need systems that make progress visible without making people feel like they're being micromanaged. Finding the right balance between transparency and autonomy is key. People need enough independence to do their best work, but enough structure that problems get identified before they become disasters.

Time zone differences add another layer of complexity. When your team spans multiple continents, there's no meeting time that works well for everyone. Someone's always joining at 6 AM or staying up until midnight. The ethical question becomes: how do you share this burden fairly? Rotating meeting times, recording important sessions, and making sure decisions don't always happen when certain team members are asleep are basic courtesies that many teams ignore.

Inclusive team dynamics aren't just about checking diversity boxes or avoiding offensive comments (though please do avoid offensive comments). It's about creating an environment where everyone feels safe contributing their ideas, even when those ideas challenge the status quo or contradict the loudest voices in the room. Some people need time to process before speaking up in meetings. Others prefer to communicate in writing. Good teams create multiple ways for people to contribute.

The most effective teams have psychological safety, meaning people can take risks, make mistakes, and voice dissenting opinions without fear of retaliation or humiliation. This doesn't mean everyone gets a participation trophy or that all ideas are equally valid. It means that when someone proposes a terrible idea, the team can discuss why it's terrible without attacking the person who suggested it.

Psychological safety starts with how leaders respond to mistakes and bad news. If your immediate reaction to problems is to find someone to blame, your team will start hiding problems until they become unfixable disasters. If your reaction is to understand what happened and figure out how to prevent it next time, people will bring you problems while they can still be solved.

Here's where team ethics get interesting: what do you do when you know a teammate is struggling but they haven't asked for help? Do you speak up and risk making them feel incompetent, or stay quiet and let them potentially fail? What about when you see someone getting overwhelmed but they keep insisting they're fine? The line between being helpful and being intrusive isn't always clear, especially when you're working remotely and can't read body language.

Conflict is inevitable in any team that's trying to accomplish something challenging. The goal isn't to avoid conflict but to make it productive. Productive conflict focuses on ideas, processes, and outcomes instead of personalities. It's the difference between "your proposal won't work because of X, Y, and Z" and "you always suggest things that won't work." One advances the conversation, the other just makes people defensive.

Managing conflict means addressing it early and directly. That passive-aggressive comment in the team chat might seem harmless, but it's usually a symptom of a bigger issue that will only get worse if ignored. Most workplace conflicts start small and escalate because nobody wants to have an uncomfortable conversation. The uncomfortable conversation is almost always easier when the problem is still small.

Cross-functional teams create their own ethical challenges. When you're working with people from different departments, you're dealing with different priorities, different success metrics, and different organizational pressures. The marketing team wants to promise features that will help close deals. The engineering team knows those features are impossible with the current timeline. The sales team just wants to know what they can tell customers. Everyone's acting rationally from their own perspective, but the team can't function if everyone only looks out for their own department.

Decision-making in teams can be painful to watch, especially when everyone's trying to reach consensus on everything. Not every decision needs input from every team member. Some decisions need one person to gather information and make a call. Others benefit from group discussion but ultimately need someone to break ties. The worst-case scenario is when teams spend hours in meetings discussing decisions that could have been made in five minutes by the person closest to the problem.

Clear roles and responsibilities prevent most team dysfunction before it starts. When everyone understands who's responsible for what, there's less confusion, less duplicated effort, and fewer things falling through the cracks. This is especially important in cross-functional teams where people have different backgrounds and might make different assumptions about who's handling what.

Here's an ethical dilemma that comes up more often than you'd think: what do you do when you're the only one who seems to care about quality? When the rest of the team is willing to ship something that's "good enough" but you know it could be better? Do you become the quality police and make everyone hate you, or do you compromise your standards to keep the peace? There's no perfect answer, but there are ways to advocate for quality without being insufferable about it.

Communication preferences vary widely, and the teams that figure this out early save themselves enormous friction. This is worth understanding at the structural level; Chapter 6 covers the practical mechanics of how to build communication systems that actually accommodate different styles.

The ethics of information sharing in teams gets complicated when different people have access to different information. Maybe you're in leadership meetings where strategic decisions get discussed. Maybe you have relationships with other teams that give you advance warning about changes. How much of this information should you share with your teammates? When does keeping information confidential cross the line into letting your team make decisions based on incomplete information?

The best teams develop their own culture and rhythms that work for their specific mix of people and challenges. They figure out how to use everyone's strengths while compensating for weaknesses. They create processes that prevent common problems without being so rigid that they can't adapt when circumstances change.

Team ethics comes down to treating your colleagues the way you'd want to be treated if your roles were reversed. Give credit generously, take responsibility for your mistakes, communicate honestly about your progress and challenges, and remember that behind every email address and video call is a real person trying to do good work.

Case Study: Google's Project Aristotle: When Data Meets Team Dynamics

Google spent years trying to figure out what made teams effective. They analyzed everything from personality types to educational backgrounds to social connections. The answer surprised them: psychological safety mattered more than individual talent.

The most successful Google teams weren't necessarily the smartest or most experienced. They were teams where people felt safe to take risks, ask questions, and admit mistakes without fear of embarrassment or punishment. Team members could disagree with each other, propose wild ideas, and acknowledge when they didn't understand something.

This validates what we discussed about creating environments where everyone feels safe contributing. The data showed that teams with psychological safety were more likely to draw on diverse perspectives, learn from failures, and deliver better results. Google's findings prove that the "soft skills" of team dynamics aren't soft at all; they're fundamental to performance.

Case Study: Spotify's Squad Model - Autonomous Teams That Work

Spotify revolutionized team structure by organizing around small, autonomous "squads" that operate like mini-startups within the larger organization. Each squad owns a piece of the product and has the authority to make decisions about how to build and improve it without waiting for approval from multiple layers of management.

The ethical foundation of Spotify's model is trust and transparency. Teams are given clear missions but freedom to determine how to achieve them. This approach respects employees' intelligence and expertise while creating accountability through results instead of micromanagement.

Squad members can move between teams based on their interests and the company's needs, preventing the stagnation and resentment that develops when people feel trapped in roles that don't suit them. This mobility creates opportunities for growth while ensuring that teams get fresh perspectives regularly.

The model works because it aligns individual autonomy with collective responsibility. Teams know they're accountable for outcomes but have the freedom to experiment, fail, and learn without bureaucratic interference. This creates genuine engagement instead of compliance-based performance.

Case Study: Yahoo's Toxic Culture - When Teams Turn Against Each Other

Yahoo's decline wasn't just about missing technological trends; it was about a culture where teams competed against each other instead of collaborating toward common goals. The company's internal politics became so toxic that employees spent more energy fighting each other than building products customers wanted.

Yahoo's stack ranking system — which Mayer inherited and maintained — forced managers to rate a certain percentage of employees as underperformers regardless of performance. This created an environment where collaboration became risky because helping colleagues could hurt your own rating. Teams hoarded information and sabotaged each other's projects.

The company's numerous reorganizations and shifting priorities meant that teams never knew if their work would survive the next executive shuffle. This uncertainty made long-term thinking impossible and encouraged short-term political maneuvering over genuine innovation.

Yahoo's acquisition by Verizon was as much about escaping the toxic culture as it was about financial necessity. The company had talented people and valuable assets but couldn't

coordinate them effectively because trust and collaboration had
been systematically destroyed.

Chapter 4: Leadership in the Modern Era

Leadership used to be easier when you could just walk around the office, see who was working and who was playing solitaire, and make decisions based on who showed up early and stayed late. Now you're trying to lead people through a screen, half your team is in different time zones, and productivity is measured by outcomes instead of how many hours someone spends looking busy at their desk.

Strip away the technology and the shifting work arrangements, and modern leadership comes down to three things: earning trust from people who have other options, making decisions with incomplete information, and creating environments where other people can do their best work. Every specific challenge in this chapter — surveillance, overpromising, delegation, managing up, handling conflict, leading through change — is really just one of these three problems wearing different clothes. The fundamental challenge of modern leadership is that you're responsible for results without having direct control over how those results get achieved. You can't hover over people's shoulders anymore (well, you could, but that would be creepy and counterproductive). This requires a completely different approach to leadership than what most managers learned when they were coming up.

Surveillance software and productivity monitoring raise serious ethical questions about trust and privacy. Just because you can track every keystroke, mouse click, and application someone uses doesn't mean you should. The temptation to monitor everything is understandable, especially when you're feeling anxious about whether remote work is working. But surveillance usually creates more problems than it solves. People find ways to game the system, and you end up measuring activity instead of productivity.

The better approach is to focus on outcomes and regular check-ins. Set clear expectations about what needs to get done and when, then trust people to figure out how to do it. If someone's consistently missing deadlines or producing poor-quality work, address that directly instead of assuming more monitoring will fix the problem.

Ethical decision-making becomes more complex when you're dealing with incomplete information and multiple stakeholders with competing interests. The customer wants features faster, your team is already stretched thin, and upper management wants to know why everything takes so long. Your job is to balance these competing demands while being honest about what's realistic and what isn't.

The pressure to overpromise is intense, especially when you're trying to keep everyone happy. Overpromising is just borrowing stress from the future. When you commit to unrealistic timelines or impossible deliverables, you're setting your team up to fail and your stakeholders up for disappointment. It feels easier in the moment to say yes to everything, but it creates bigger problems down the road.

Leading in a flattened hierarchy means you can't rely on formal authority to get things done. People have more options now. If they don't like working for you, they can find another job, start freelancing, or transfer to a different team. Your leadership has to be based on influence and trust instead of position and power.

This shift requires different skills than traditional command-and-control leadership. You need to be better at persuasion, better at building consensus, and better at creating environments where people want to do their best work. You can't just tell people what to do; you have to help them understand why it matters and how it fits into the bigger picture.

The hardest part of leadership is making decisions with imperfect information under time pressure. You rarely have all the facts you'd like, and waiting for more information often means missing opportunities or letting problems get worse. Learning to make good decisions quickly with incomplete data is one of the most valuable leadership skills you can develop.

Sometimes the ethical choice conflicts with what seems like the practical choice. Maybe you know that laying off a struggling team member would improve overall team performance, but you also know they're dealing with personal challenges that are affecting their work. Maybe you could win a big contract by making promises you're not sure you can keep. Maybe you could motivate your team by taking credit for work they did. The easy choice isn't always the right choice.

The weight of leadership communication is something most new managers underestimate. People parse your words carefully, looking for hints about strategy, job security, and organizational priorities. A casual comment about exploring new directions can spark rumors about layoffs. An offhand criticism of a competitor can be interpreted as a change in company strategy. You have to be more thoughtful about what you say and how you say it.

Managing up presents its own ethical challenges. Your boss wants optimistic updates and confident projections. Your team needs realistic timelines and adequate resources. When these two needs conflict, you're caught in the middle. Do you tell your boss what they want to hear and hope things work out? Do you advocate aggressively for your team and risk being seen as negative or uncooperative? The answer usually involves finding ways to be honest about challenges while also presenting solutions.

Resource allocation is where leadership ethics get really tested. You never have enough budget, enough time, or enough people to do everything everyone wants. Every decision to fund one project means another project doesn't get resources. Every decision to assign your best people to one initiative means other initiatives get your second-string players. These zero-sum decisions force you to make choices about priorities that affect real people's careers and livelihoods.

The ethics of performance management go beyond just being fair in evaluations. It's about creating systems that help people succeed instead of just measuring whether they're succeeding. This means providing clear expectations, regular feedback, opportunities for development, and support when people are struggling. It also means having difficult conversations early instead of letting problems fester until they become termination issues.

Layoffs and reorganizations are the ultimate test of leadership ethics. When business conditions force you to eliminate positions, how do you decide who stays and who goes? How do you communicate these decisions to the people affected and the people who remain? How do you maintain team morale and productivity while dealing with the guilt and stress of making these choices?

The temptation during difficult times is to avoid transparency because you think it will create panic or hurt morale. People usually handle bad news better than they handle uncertainty. If budget cuts are coming, if projects are being canceled, if roles are being eliminated, address it directly. People can make better decisions about their own careers when they have accurate information about what's happening.

Leading through change means constantly asking people to adapt to new tools, new processes, and new ways of working. Change is exhausting, and people have limited capacity for it. Good leaders help their teams prioritize which changes are essential and which can wait. They also recognize that change affects different people differently and provide support for those who struggle with transitions.

Delegation reveals a lot about a leader's character. The temptation is to keep the interesting, high-visibility work for yourself and delegate the boring, tedious stuff to your team. Good delegation means giving people opportunities to grow and develop new skills, even if that means letting them work on projects you'd enjoy doing yourself. It also means accepting that they might do things differently than you would, and that's okay as long as they get good results.

The most challenging ethical dilemmas in leadership involve competing loyalties. Your responsibility to your team might conflict with your responsibility to the organization. Your short-term obligations might conflict with strategy. Your personal values might conflict with company policies. Learning to navigate these conflicts without compromising your integrity is the essence of ethical leadership.

Power dynamics create blind spots that can undermine even well-intentioned leaders. When you're in charge, people are less likely to give you honest feedback, challenge your ideas, or tell you when you're wrong. Creating channels for upward feedback and criticism requires intentional effort and genuine receptiveness to hearing things you might not want to hear.

The best leaders are the ones people choose to follow, not the ones people have to follow. In a world where talented people have more options than ever, earning that choice every day is both the challenge and the privilege of modern leadership. Your job is to remove obstacles so your team can do their best work, provide them with the resources and information they need to succeed, and create an environment where people feel valued and supported.

Leadership is about serving others instead of being served. When you succeed as a leader, it's because your team succeeds, not the other way around.

Case Study: Reed Hastings and Netflix: Radical Transparency in Leadership

When Netflix CEO Reed Hastings published his culture memo, he wasn't just creating internal policy; he was demonstrating a new approach to leadership transparency. The memo introduced a core management question — would you fight to keep this person on your team? — which Netflix called the "keeper test," and outlined their philosophy of "freedom and responsibility."

Hastings' approach illustrates the modern leadership challenge of being honest about difficult decisions while maintaining team morale. He openly discussed firing practices, performance expectations, and the reality that Netflix wasn't a "family" but a professional sports team where performance mattered.

This transparency created clarity about expectations but also generated controversy about corporate culture. Hastings had to balance honesty with empathy, showing how modern leaders must navigate competing demands for authenticity and inclusivity while making tough business decisions.

Case Study: Patagonia's Yvon Chouinard - Values-Driven Leadership

Yvon Chouinard built Patagonia around the principle that business should serve environmental protection instead of just profit maximization. His leadership demonstrates how authentic values can create sustainable competitive advantages while contributing to social good.

Chouinard's decision to donate the company to environmental causes instead of selling it or going public shows leadership that prioritizes mission over personal wealth. This choice aligns with decades of decisions that sometimes hurt short-term profits but built long-term brand loyalty and employee engagement.

The company's activism on environmental issues isn't just marketing; it's integrated into business operations through supply chain requirements, product design decisions, and political advocacy. Employees know their work contributes to causes they care about, creating engagement that goes beyond paychecks.

Patagonia's leadership development focuses on environmental stewardship and social responsibility alongside business skills. The company treats leadership as service to the mission instead of personal advancement, creating a culture where power is used responsibly.

Case Study: Travis Kalanick's Uber - Charismatic Leadership Gone Wrong

Travis Kalanick's leadership of Uber illustrates how charismatic leaders can create massive value while causing enormous damage through unethical decision-making and toxic culture creation. His aggressive "win at all costs" mentality built a global company but ultimately made his own leadership position unsustainable.

Kalanick's approach to regulation was ethically problematic because it treated laws as suggestions instead of requirements. Uber entered markets without permission, operated illegally, and used political pressure to change regulations after the fact. This approach normalized lawbreaking throughout the organization.

The culture Kalanick created valued growth and disruption over employee welfare and ethical business practices. Sexual harassment, discrimination, and toxic management became widespread because leadership signaled that results mattered more than methods.

Kalanick's eventual resignation shows how unethical leadership eventually becomes self-defeating. The culture he created damaged the company's reputation, triggered regulatory backlash, and made it impossible for him to lead the company through the next phase of its development.

Chapter 5: Addressing Problematic Behavior

Every workplace has that one person. You know the one. They might be the colleague who takes credit for other people's ideas, the manager who throws tantrums when things don't go their way, or the team member who somehow manages to create drama wherever they go. The question isn't whether you'll encounter problematic behavior at work (you will), but how you'll handle it when you do.

We're not talking about normal workplace friction here. This isn't about the colleague who chews too loudly or the manager who schedules too many meetings. This is about behavior that crosses lines, undermines others, or creates genuinely toxic work environments. The kind of behavior that makes people dread coming to work, affects their performance, or drives good employees to quit.

The tricky part about addressing serious problematic behavior is that it often masquerades as normal workplace challenges. The manager who systematically undermines certain employees while praising others. The colleague who sabotages projects to make themselves look better. The team member who spreads rumors and creates divisions between coworkers. These people are often skilled at making their behavior look like standard office politics or personality conflicts.

Gaslighting is insidious because it's designed to make you question your own perception of reality. The person will deny things they clearly said or did, claim you're being too sensitive, or insist that you're misunderstanding their intentions. They're expert at making you feel like you're the problem for noticing their problematic behavior.

Recognizing workplace toxicity starts with trusting your instincts when something feels consistently wrong. If you find yourself constantly second-guessing your interactions with a person, if you're walking on eggshells around them, or if you notice other people avoiding them, pay attention to those signals. Toxic people create patterns of discomfort and dysfunction that extend beyond normal workplace disagreements.

Manipulation tactics in the workplace can be subtle but devastating. The colleague who volunteers you for extra work without asking, then acts like they're doing you a favor. The manager who gives you impossible deadlines and then blames you when you can't meet them. The team member who shares confidential information about others to build alliances and gather intelligence.

Credit theft is more common than people realize and can be damaging to careers. It might be someone who presents your ideas as their own in meetings, takes over your projects and minimizes your contributions, or subtly suggests that they were responsible for successes you achieved. This behavior is often gradual and calculated, making it hard to address without looking petty.

Workplace bullying by adults is real and can be just as damaging as childhood bullying. It might involve public humiliation, deliberate exclusion from important communications, setting someone up to fail, or using authority to make someone's work life miserable. The target often feels isolated because they're afraid of being seen as weak or unable to handle normal workplace challenges.

Power dynamics make addressing problematic behavior challenging when the person causing problems has more authority than you do. The boss who plays favorites, makes unreasonable demands, or creates hostile environments for certain employees. The senior colleague who undermines junior staff or uses their influence to protect themselves from consequences.

Documentation becomes critical when dealing with serious problematic behavior, not just for potential legal protection but to maintain your own sanity. Keep detailed records of incidents with dates, times, witnesses, and examples. This helps counter gaslighting attempts and provides concrete evidence if you need to escalate.

Witnesses are your best allies when dealing with toxic behavior. Problematic people often behave differently when others are watching, so having witnesses to incidents is crucial. They can also provide support when you're questioning whether something happened the way you remember it.

HR departments vary wildly in their competence and willingness to address serious problematic behavior. Some are genuinely focused on creating healthy work environments. Others are concerned with protecting the company from liability and will only act when forced to. Knowing which type you're dealing with helps set appropriate expectations.

Retaliation is a real risk when you report or confront problematic behavior. The person might try to make your work life more difficult, exclude you from opportunities, or even try to get you fired. This is why documentation and building alliances with colleagues and management are so important before you escalate.

Serial problematic employees often have a pattern of causing issues wherever they go. They might have a trail of former colleagues who left because of them, a history of teams that underperformed while they were involved, or a reputation for being "difficult" that management tolerates because they produce results or have valuable skills.

Protecting yourself sometimes means strategic disengagement instead of direct confrontation. Limit your interactions with the problematic person to necessary work communications. Avoid being alone with them. Keep interactions professional and documented. Don't share personal information that could be used against you later.

When problematic behavior involves discrimination, harassment, or illegal activities, the situation becomes more serious and requires immediate escalation. This isn't about personality conflicts or management style differences. This is about behavior that violates laws and policies and can expose both you and the company to significant liability.

Coalitions with other affected colleagues can be powerful but require careful coordination. Multiple voices reporting similar patterns of behavior are harder to dismiss than isolated complaints. But be careful about how you approach this to avoid looking like you're organizing against someone or creating drama.

Sometimes the most ethical choice is to remove yourself from the situation entirely. This might mean transferring to a different team, finding a new job, or declining to work on projects with the problematic person. This isn't giving up; it's recognizing that some people won't change and some situations can't be fixed.

Exit interviews can be an opportunity to document problematic behavior for the record, especially if you're leaving because of it. Be factual about incidents and their impact. Even if nothing changes immediately, your feedback might be the final piece that helps management recognize a pattern.

The impact of toxic behavior extends far beyond the direct targets. It affects team morale, productivity, and retention. It drives away good employees and creates environments where problematic behavior becomes normalized. Someone has to be willing to address it, even when it's difficult and risky.

Legal protections exist for certain types of problematic behavior, when it involves discrimination, harassment, or retaliation for reporting illegal activities. Understanding your rights and the proper channels for reporting can help you navigate serious situations more effectively.

The goal isn't to become the workplace ethics police or to escalate every interpersonal conflict. The goal is to recognize when behavior crosses lines from normal workplace friction into genuinely problematic territory and to respond appropriately to protect yourself and your colleagues.

Addressing serious problematic behavior is about refusing to normalize toxicity. When bad behavior goes unchallenged, it gets worse and spreads. When people are held accountable for their actions, it creates better environments for everyone. Someone has to be willing to speak up, and that someone might need to be you.

Case Study: Uber and the Fowler memo: documentation as a force multiplier

Kalanick's Uber was covered in the previous chapter as a leadership failure. Its relevance here is more specific: former engineer Susan Fowler's 2017 blog post demonstrated how a single, well-documented firsthand account could force accountability that years of internal complaints had failed to produce.

Fowler had reported harassment to HR multiple times. HR had done nothing. What changed wasn't the severity of the behavior — it was the documentation. Her post was specific, timestamped, and impossible to dismiss as a personal grievance. The detail gave it weight. Within months of publication, Kalanick resigned and an independent investigation confirmed systemic problems across the organization.

The takeaway for people dealing with problematic behavior: documentation is not just legal protection. It's the difference between a complaint that can be minimized and a record that cannot.

Case Study: Google's Handling of Andy Rubin - Protecting the Powerful

Google's handling of Android creator Andy Rubin's sexual misconduct allegations shows how even companies with strong stated values can fail when problematic behavior involves powerful executives. The company paid Rubin a $90 million exit package despite credible allegations of inappropriate conduct.

The ethical failure wasn't just in the original misconduct but in Google's response to it. By providing a generous exit package and allowing Rubin to leave quietly, the company prioritized reputation management over accountability and justice for affected employees.

Google employees organized walkouts to protest the company's handling of sexual harassment cases, demanding transparency about executive misconduct and equal treatment regardless of seniority. The employee activism forced leadership to confront how their policies protected powerful people at the expense of vulnerable employees.

The incident damaged Google's credibility on workplace equity and inclusion issues. The company's public statements about creating safe workplaces were undermined by private actions that showed different standards for different employees based on their power and value to the organization.

Case Study: Buffer's Transparent Response to Harassment Allegations

When Buffer faced harassment allegations against a senior employee, the company's response demonstrated how to address problematic behavior transparently and fairly. The social media company conducted a thorough investigation and publicly shared their findings and corrective actions.

Buffer's commitment to transparency meant sharing details about their investigation process, the actions they took, and the policy changes they implemented to prevent similar problems. This approach prioritized accountability over reputation management and showed genuine commitment to creating a safe workplace.

The company used the incident as an opportunity to examine their entire culture and make systemic improvements instead of just addressing the individual case. They implemented new training, updated policies, and created better reporting mechanisms based on what they learned from the investigation.

Buffer's handling of the situation built instead of damaged employee trust because people saw that the company would take difficult action when necessary and learn from mistakes instead of covering them up.

Chapter 6: Communication Excellence

Communication in the modern workplace has gotten about as complicated as trying to explain TikTok to your grandmother. We've moved beyond the simple challenge of coordinating teams to navigating a maze of platforms, protocols, and unspoken rules that can make or break your professional reputation. The way you communicate has become as important as what you communicate.

Every message you send, every email you write, and every comment you make in meetings becomes part of your professional brand. Your communication style signals competence, reliability, and judgment in ways that your work output might not. People form opinions about your capabilities based on whether you can write a clear subject line or explain complex ideas without jargon.

Email etiquette reveals more about someone's professionalism than most people realize. The colleague who sends emails with no subject line, the manager who writes novels when a sentence would suffice, and the team member who hits reply-all to say "thanks" are all broadcasting information about their judgment and consideration for others.

Subject line discipline is apparently too much to ask for in most organizations. "Quick question" tells me nothing useful. "Update" could mean anything from "we're ahead of schedule" to "the building is on fire." "Following up" makes me want to hide under my desk because it usually means someone wants something I forgot to do and is being passive-aggressive about reminding me.

The carbon copy function has created a whole new category of workplace politics. Who gets cc'd on emails has become a signal about hierarchy, inclusion, and information access that has nothing to do with who needs the information. Using cc strategically to cover yourself or demonstrate importance is manipulative. Using it thoughtlessly creates noise and confusion.

Professional writing skills have become more important as communication has become more text-based, but somehow writing quality has gotten worse. People send messages that would embarrass a middle school student, use emoji in client communications, and seem to think that "professional" means using unnecessarily complex language that obscures meaning.

Tone is nearly impossible to convey in written communication, leading to misunderstandings and hurt feelings. That message you thought was friendly and casual might come across as curt or dismissive to the recipient. The joke that seemed harmless in your head might offend someone who doesn't share your sense of humor or cultural context.

Information hierarchy becomes crucial when you're communicating with people at different levels of the organization. The detailed technical explanation that's perfect for your peer might be overwhelming for a senior executive who just needs the bottom line. The high-level summary that works for leadership might leave your implementation team without enough detail to do the work.

Instant messaging platforms have created an expectation of immediate response that's both unrealistic and unsustainable. Just because someone can reach you instantly doesn't mean they should expect instant answers to non-urgent questions. The pressure to be constantly available creates stress and interrupts deep work, but the social expectation to respond quickly makes it hard to set boundaries.

Platform confusion is rampant in organizations that use multiple communication tools without clear protocols about which tool serves what purpose. Important decisions get lost in casual chat threads, urgent messages get buried in email chains, and critical information gets scattered across platforms where not everyone can access it.

Response time management requires setting and communicating boundaries about availability and urgency. Not every message deserves an immediate response, and not every question constitutes an emergency. Learning to triage communications and respond appropriately based on priority instead of perceived urgency is a crucial professional skill.

Communication overload is the flip side of having better tools. When everyone can reach everyone else all the time through multiple channels, the volume becomes overwhelming. People start ignoring messages, missing important information, and feeling anxious about falling behind on their digital communications.

Clarity versus diplomacy creates constant tension in professional communication. Sometimes being direct and clear conflicts with being polite and diplomatic. The challenge is learning when to prioritize clarity and when to prioritize relationship maintenance, and how to achieve both when possible.

Audience awareness becomes complex when the same message might be read by your boss, your peer, your client, and your intern, all of whom will interpret it differently based on their relationship with you and their understanding of the situation. Writing for multiple audiences simultaneously is challenging and often results in messages that satisfy no one.

Professional boundaries in communication include knowing what information to share with whom, understanding the appropriate level of formality for different relationships, and recognizing when personal and professional communication should be kept separate.

Feedback delivery through digital channels requires extra care because you lose all the nonverbal cues that help soften criticism and ensure understanding. Critical feedback that might be well-received in person can come across as harsh or unfair in writing.

Meeting communication has its own set of rules and expectations. Knowing when to speak up, how to disagree respectfully, when to ask clarifying questions, and how to contribute meaningfully without dominating the conversation are skills that affect how others perceive your competence and collaboration ability.

Client communication carries higher stakes because external relationships are often more fragile than internal ones. The informal tone that works with colleagues might seem unprofessional to clients. The detailed explanations that satisfy internal stakeholders might overwhelm external partners who just want to know if you're on track.

Crisis communication tests all your other communication skills under pressure. When things go wrong, how you communicate about the problem, what information you share and when, and how you balance transparency with discretion can determine whether a crisis gets resolved or escalated.

Good communication in the modern workplace requires being intentional about your word choices, understanding your audience, and recognizing that how you say something often matters more than what you say. Your communication style becomes part of your professional reputation, so it's worth investing the time to get it right.

The ethics of communication boil down to being honest about what you know and don't know, being clear about expectations and deadlines, and being respectful of other people's time and attention. It means not using communication tools to avoid accountability, create confusion, or manipulate situations to your advantage.

Case Study: Buffer's radical transparency: two sides of the same coin

Buffer appeared in the previous chapter for how it handled harassment allegations — transparently, with published investigation findings and policy changes. That same transparency-first culture shows up differently in their communication philosophy: the company shares employee salaries, revenue figures, and internal discussions publicly.

The two examples together illustrate something important. Radical transparency works when it's applied consistently, not just when it's convenient. Buffer's willingness to be open about internal misconduct was credible precisely because openness was already their default, not a one-time PR response.

The flip side is that extreme transparency creates its own pressures — employees can't keep professional information private, and constant visibility can feel like being permanently on message. More communication isn't always better communication, and good intentions can create unintended consequences when taken to extremes.

Slack practices what it preaches about communication by using its own platform for radical internal transparency. Most company communications happen in public channels where any employee can see discussions about strategy, performance, and decision-making.

This transparency creates accountability because leaders know their communications will be visible to the entire organization. It also reduces rumors and speculation because employees have access to real information about what's happening and why decisions are being made.

The company has developed sophisticated norms about when to use public versus private channels, how to handle sensitive information, and how to maintain productive dialogue when disagreements arise. These norms make transparency practical instead of chaotic.

Slack's approach shows how technology can enable better communication practices when it's combined with clear cultural expectations about openness, respect, and constructive dialogue.

Case Study: Basecamp's Communication Meltdown

Basecamp's 2021 decision to ban political discussions at work triggered a communication crisis that ultimately led to the departure of a third of their employees. The company's handling of employee concerns showed how poor communication can escalate workplace tensions instead of resolving them.

The initial policy announcement was made unilaterally without employee input, and leadership's subsequent communications were defensive and dismissive of employee concerns. Instead of creating dialogue about workplace boundaries, the approach shut down conversation and created resentment.

When employees raised concerns about the policy's impact on inclusion and psychological safety, leadership responded with additional restrictions instead of addressing the underlying issues. This pattern of communication showed that employee input wasn't genuinely valued.

The mass exodus of employees demonstrated that communication failures can have severe business consequences. Basecamp lost institutional knowledge, damaged its reputation as an employer, and faced challenges rebuilding trust with remaining employees.

Chapter 7: Digital Presence and Social Media

Your digital footprint used to be something only celebrities and politicians worried about. Now everyone's online presence can make or break careers, and the line between personal and professional has gotten blurrier than a video call with bad internet. What you post, like, share, and comment on can follow you for your entire career, and deleting something doesn't make it disappear when screenshots exist.

Social media platforms were designed for personal sharing, not professional networking, but they've become crucial for career development whether we like it or not. LinkedIn is supposed to be the professional platform, but it's turned into a weird hybrid of resume bragging and motivational quotes that would make a life coach cringe. Meanwhile, platforms like LinkedIn, Instagram, and whatever has replaced Twitter this week have become informal networking tools where industry conversations happen in real-time.

Professional social media guidelines vary wildly between companies and industries. Some organizations have detailed policies about what employees can and can't post. Others operate on the assumption that what you do on your own time is your business, right up until it becomes their business because you've embarrassed the company or violated client confidentiality.

The ethics of personal branding start with the question of authenticity versus marketability. How much of your real personality should you show online? Is it okay to present a curated version of yourself that emphasizes your professional strengths while downplaying your flaws and struggles? Everyone's doing it, but that doesn't make it honest or healthy.

LinkedIn has created a culture of professional performance that can be exhausting to maintain. People share inspirational stories about overcoming challenges, celebrate every minor achievement, and post motivational content that sounds like it was written by a corporate consultant on caffeine. The pressure to constantly demonstrate professional growth and positive attitude can make the platform feel like a never-ending job interview.

Company representation becomes complicated when your personal social media presence is tied to your professional identity. Even if your bio says "views are my own," everyone knows where you work. Your opinions, jokes, and political views reflect on your employer whether you intend them to or not. How much of your personal expression are you willing to sacrifice for professional safety?

Privacy settings are your first line of defense, but they're not foolproof. Platform privacy policies change, account security can be compromised, and what's private today might become public tomorrow. The safer approach is to assume that anything you post online could eventually become public and post accordingly.

The temptation to overshare is real, especially on platforms that reward engagement. Personal struggles, family drama, health issues, financial problems, and relationship troubles might generate sympathy and comments, but they can also make colleagues and clients uncomfortable or question your judgment and stability.

Professional networking through social media requires a different approach than personal socializing. The goal is to build relationships that could benefit your career, but doing it in a way that feels authentic instead of transactional. Nobody likes the person who only reaches out when they need something, but everyone appreciates someone who shares interesting content and engages thoughtfully with others' posts.

Industry conversations on social media can be valuable for staying current with trends and building your reputation as someone who understands your field. But they can also be minefields of controversy, insider politics, and virtue signaling. Knowing when to engage and when to stay silent is a skill that comes with experience and occasional mistakes.

Political expression online is where many professionals get into trouble. Your political views are your right, but expressing them publicly can alienate colleagues, clients, and potential employers who disagree. The question isn't whether you should have political opinions, but whether expressing them online is worth the potential professional consequences.

AI tools and content creation ethics have added a new layer of complexity to social media. Is it okay to use ChatGPT to write your LinkedIn posts? Should you disclose when images have been AI-generated? What about using automation tools to schedule posts or engagement? The rules are still being written, but transparency is usually the safer approach.

Client connections on social media create boundary issues that didn't exist when professional relationships were more clearly separated from personal ones. Should you connect with clients on LinkedIn? What about following them on Instagram? How do you handle it when clients want to connect on platforms where you share personal content?

The permanence of digital content means that jokes, opinions, and photos from years ago can resurface at inconvenient times. That edgy post from college, the party photos from your twenties, or the political rant from last year could become problems when you're applying for new jobs or trying to advance your career.

Content moderation and platform algorithms affect what people see of your posts, but they're opaque and constantly changing. A post that would have been seen by hundreds of your connections last year might only reach a handful today. Understanding how these systems work (to the extent anyone does) can help you communicate more effectively.

Professional photography and visual presentation matter more than ever in a world where video calls and profile pictures are often people's first impression of you. The selfie that looks fine on your phone might not work for a LinkedIn profile. The background visible in your video calls sends messages about your professionalism and attention to detail.

Crisis management for social media involves knowing how to respond when posts go wrong or when you become the target of online criticism. Sometimes the best response is no response. Other times, a quick apology and correction can prevent a small mistake from becoming a bigger problem. Understanding the difference requires good judgment and sometimes advice from people outside the situation.

Cross-platform consistency matters when your professional identity spans multiple social media platforms. The persona you present on LinkedIn should be recognizable as the same person on Twitter, even if the tone and content are different. Dramatic inconsistencies can make you seem unreliable or inauthentic.

The ethics of engagement include how you interact with other people's content. Do you like posts you don't agree with just to maintain relationships? Do you share content without reading it carefully? Do you engage with controversial topics in ways that add value to the conversation or just increase the noise?

Digital wellness becomes important when social media starts affecting your mental health or consuming too much of your time and attention. The dopamine hits from likes and comments can be addictive, and the comparison culture of social media can make everyone else's career look more successful than your own.

Your digital presence is part of your professional toolkit whether you manage it or not. The choice isn't whether to have an online presence, but whether to be intentional about what that presence communicates about your judgment, values, and competence. In a world where people Google your name before meeting you, your digital footprint might be making first impressions before you ever get the chance to.

Case Study: James Damore's Google Memo: When Personal Views Meet Professional Consequences

James Damore's internal memo questioning Google's diversity initiatives became a lightning rod for debates about workplace political expression. His firing demonstrated how personal viewpoints shared in professional contexts can have career-ending consequences, regardless of the author's intentions.

The incident illustrates the challenge of balancing free expression with inclusive workplace environments. Damore believed he was contributing to internal debate about company policies. Critics argued his memo created a hostile environment for women colleagues. Google concluded his views were incompatible with their values.

This case shows how the line between personal opinion and professional conduct has become increasingly blurred, especially when internal communications can become public. It demonstrates why understanding your company's values and the potential reach of your communications matters more than ever.

Case Study: Ben & Jerry's Authentic Social Media Activism

Ben & Jerry's uses social media to advocate for social justice causes in ways that align with the company's values and history of activism. Their approach shows how organizations can engage in political discourse authentically while maintaining business relationships.

The company's social media activism isn't performative because it's backed by concrete actions: policy advocacy, financial contributions to causes, and business practices that support their stated values. This alignment between online communication and real-world behavior creates credibility.

Ben & Jerry's accepts that their activism may alienate some customers and business partners, but they maintain their positions because they're grounded in genuine convictions instead of marketing calculations. This authentic approach builds stronger relationships with aligned stakeholders.

The company's long history of activism means their social media presence feels consistent instead of opportunistic. They've built audience expectations around their values-driven communications, making political content feel natural instead of surprising.

Case Study: Palmer Luckey's Political Donations Controversy

Oculus founder Palmer Luckey's financial support for anti-Hillary Clinton memes during the 2016 election created controversy that ultimately contributed to his departure from Facebook. His case illustrates how personal political activities can affect professional relationships even when they occur outside work.

Luckey's support for the "Nimble America" organization became public when journalists investigated the group's funding sources. His political activities weren't illegal or explicitly related to his work, but they created tensions with colleagues and damaged his relationship with Facebook leadership.

The controversy divided employees and created an uncomfortable work environment where Luckey's political views became a daily source of tension. Facebook faced pressure from employees who opposed his political activities and from conservatives who saw his treatment as political discrimination.

Luckey's eventual departure showed how digital trails make private political activities public and how political polarization can make it difficult for people with controversial views to maintain professional relationships regardless of their job performance.

Chapter 8: Managing Time and Expectations

Time management used to be about prioritizing tasks and avoiding procrastination. Now it's about juggling competing deadlines across multiple projects while trying to maintain the illusion that you're productive but not overwhelmed, available but not desperate, and always meeting expectations that seem to change daily.

The ethics of time management start with being honest about what you can accomplish in the time available. The temptation to overcommit is intense, especially when saying no might disappoint people or make you look like you're not a team player. But consistently overpromising and underdelivering is worse than being realistic about your capacity from the start.

Deadline estimation is where most people's optimism gets them into trouble. We consistently underestimate how long tasks will take because we plan for the best-case scenario where nothing goes wrong, no one asks for revisions, and all the dependencies align perfectly. Then reality hits, and suddenly that "quick project" has consumed two weeks and derailed three other commitments.

The planning fallacy affects everyone, but it's problematic in workplace settings where your bad estimates affect other people's schedules. When you tell someone their project will take two weeks but it takes four, you're not just managing your own time poorly; you're sabotaging their planning and creating cascade effects throughout the organization.

Capacity management means understanding not just how many hours you have available, but what kind of work you can realistically do in those hours. An hour spent in back-to-back meetings is not equivalent to an hour of focused work time. An hour spent on creative projects when you're mentally exhausted is not equivalent to an hour spent on routine tasks when you're fresh.

The ethics of saying no involve being honest about your limitations while offering alternatives when possible. Instead of just declining requests, consider whether you can suggest different timelines, reduced scope, or other people who might be able to help. The goal is to be helpful while protecting your ability to deliver quality work on existing commitments.

Project triage becomes necessary when you have more commitments than capacity. Not all projects are equally important, and not all deadlines are equally firm. Learning to identify which work has real consequences if delayed and which work is just someone's preference helps you allocate time more effectively and communicate priorities clearly.

Scope creep happens gradually and often unintentionally, but it can destroy carefully planned timelines. The "quick addition" that seems minor can cascade into significant delays when it requires additional research, approvals, or coordination. Learning to identify and address scope changes protects both project timelines and your sanity.

Planning as if everything will go perfectly is setting yourself up for disappointment. Build time for the inevitable obstacles, the revision round nobody budgeted, and the coordination that always takes twice as long as expected.

The overcommitment trap is dangerous for people who want to be seen as helpful and capable. Taking on too many projects doesn't make you look productive; it makes you look disorganized when you start missing deadlines and delivering subpar work. Better to do fewer things well than many things poorly.

Deadline negotiation is often possible but requires early communication and alternative solutions. Most people would rather adjust timeline expectations than receive poor-quality work delivered on the original deadline. But this only works if you identify problems early enough that adjustments are still possible.

Priority conflicts are inevitable when you're working on multiple projects with different stakeholders who all consider their work the most important. The key is having transparent conversations about competing deadlines and getting clear guidance about which projects take precedence when conflicts arise.

Personal productivity systems become crucial when you're managing complex, interconnected responsibilities. Whether you use sophisticated project management software or simple to-do lists, having a system that works for you and that others can understand when necessary helps ensure nothing falls through the cracks.

The myth of multitasking continues to persist despite overwhelming evidence that it reduces both quality and efficiency. The constant switching between tasks creates mental fatigue and increases the likelihood of mistakes. Protecting blocks of focused time for important work often requires defending your calendar against non-essential meetings and interruptions.

Workload visibility helps both you and your colleagues make better decisions about new commitments. When people can see what you're already working on, they're more likely to understand why you can't take on additional projects or why certain requests might take longer than expected.

Emergency versus preference is a distinction that gets lost when everything is treated as urgent. True emergencies are rare, but the culture of urgency makes every request feel like it needs immediate attention. Developing the judgment to distinguish between what's urgent and what's just someone's preference is crucial for maintaining sanity and effectiveness.

Time tracking, whether formal or informal, helps create realistic expectations for future projects. Most people underestimate how long tasks take, partly because they forget about interruptions, revisions, and coordination time. Keeping track of time spent helps improve future planning and provides data for timeline discussions.

The ethics of estimation involve being honest about uncertainty instead of giving false precision. Saying "this will take between three and five days depending on how the research goes" is more honest than saying "this will take four days" when you're really just guessing.

Seasonal and cyclical workloads affect most businesses but are often ignored in planning processes. Budget cycles, fiscal year-ends, holiday seasons, and industry-specific busy periods create predictable crunch times that should be factored into project timelines instead of treated as surprises.

Deadline padding has become a defensive mechanism for people who have been burned by unrealistic timelines. Building in extra time protects against unexpected delays, but it can also create inefficiency if everyone is padding their estimates and no one is working with accurate information about requirements.

The opportunity cost of overcommitment includes not just the work you can't do well, but the stress, health impacts, and relationship strain that come from constantly running behind. Sometimes the most ethical choice is to protect your capacity so you can deliver quality work on the commitments you do make.

Personal sustainability means recognizing that consistently working at maximum capacity is unsustainable and counterproductive. Burnout doesn't just affect you; it affects everyone who depends on your work. Sustainable work practices are an ethical obligation to yourself and your colleagues.

Managing time and expectations ethically means being honest about what you can deliver, when you can deliver it, and what resources you need to do it well. It means making realistic commitments and communicating proactively when circumstances change. Most importantly, it means recognizing that good time management isn't about doing more things faster, but about doing the right things well with realistic timelines that allow for quality work and sustainable effort.

Case Study: Basecamp's Approach: The Ethics of Saying No

Basecamp, the project management software company, built their business model around helping teams do less but do it better. Their philosophy challenges the culture of overcommitment that plagues most organizations.

Founders Jason Fried and David Heinemeier Hansson advocate for 40-hour work weeks, realistic project timelines, and saying no to opportunities that would stretch teams too thin. They argue that sustainable productivity requires protecting capacity instead of maximizing it.

Their approach demonstrates the ethical dimension of time management: being honest about what's achievable, protecting team wellbeing over short-term gains, and recognizing that overcommitment ultimately hurts everyone involved. Basecamp shows that saying no can be a competitive advantage instead of a limitation.

Case Study: Asana's No Meeting Wednesdays

Asana implemented "No Meeting Wednesdays" to protect employees' deep work time and demonstrate organizational commitment to sustainable productivity. The policy shows how companies can set boundaries that benefit both individual performance and collective results.

The policy works because it's enforced consistently across all levels of the organization, including executives who model the behavior they expect from others. This consistency prevents the policy from becoming just another rule that important people ignore.

Asana measures the impact of meeting-free time on productivity and employee satisfaction, using data to refine their approach and demonstrate that time protection creates instead of reduces value. This evidence-based approach helps sustain commitment to the policy.

The company uses the protected time to focus on strategic thinking, creative work, and individual productivity instead of just catching up on email or administrative tasks. This intentional use of time makes the policy genuinely valuable instead of just symbolic.

Case Study: Amazon's Unrealistic Delivery Promises

Amazon's increasingly aggressive delivery timeframes create ethical problems when the company promises customers delivery times that can only be achieved by pushing warehouse and delivery workers beyond reasonable limits.

The company's same-day and one-day delivery promises often require workers to skip breaks, work overtime, and prioritize speed over safety. These working conditions aren't sustainable and create physical and psychological stress that affects worker health and family relationships.

Amazon's delivery time commitments also create problems for logistics partners who must choose between maintaining humane working conditions and meeting contract requirements. This pressure pushes ethical problems throughout the supply chain.

The company's focus on delivery speed comes at the expense of long-term sustainability and worker welfare. While customers appreciate fast delivery, the hidden costs in human suffering and environmental impact make the promises ethically questionable.

Chapter 9: Integrity in Action

Integrity used to be simpler when work was mostly about showing up, doing your job, and not stealing office supplies. Now it's about navigating a world where your work might be done by AI, your data is stored in the cloud by companies you've never heard of, and half your colleagues are contractors who might be working for your competitors next month.

The challenge with modern integrity is that the rules aren't clearly defined, the consequences aren't immediately obvious, and the temptations are everywhere. It's easier than ever to cut corners, fudge numbers, or take credit for work that isn't entirely yours. It's also easier to get caught, thanks to digital trails that preserve everything forever.

Honesty in remote work environments requires a different kind of discipline than in-person honesty. When your boss can't see what you're doing, the temptation to multitask during meetings, exaggerate your progress on projects, or take longer breaks than you should becomes much stronger. The lack of direct supervision tests whether your work ethic is genuine or just performed for an audience.

The ethics of productivity reporting get murky when you're working from home. Do you count the time you spent thinking about a problem while walking your dog? What about the brilliant idea you had in the shower? How do you track time when your most productive hours might be outside traditional business hours, and your least productive time might be during scheduled work time?

Intellectual property in the age of AI has created new ethical gray areas that prior generations of workers never faced. If you use ChatGPT to help write a proposal, do you need to disclose that? If you use AI to generate images for a presentation, who owns the copyright? If an AI tool helps you debug code, are you still the author of the solution?

The temptation to use AI as a shortcut is understandable, especially when deadlines are tight and the technology is readily available. But there's a difference between using AI as a tool to enhance your work and using it to replace your thinking entirely. The ethical line is somewhere between helpful assistance and academic dishonesty, but that line isn't clearly marked.

AI attribution becomes complicated when the technology is integrated into the tools you use every day. Your word processor suggests edits, your email client drafts responses, your coding environment autocompletes functions. At what point does assistance become authorship? The industry hasn't settled on clear standards, leaving everyone to figure out their own ethical boundaries.

Financial ethics have expanded beyond not embezzling money to include expense reporting, time tracking, and resource usage. The company credit card that you use for business travel can also buy personal items. The software license that your company pays for can also be used for personal projects. The home office that you claim on your taxes is also where you play video games.

Expense gray areas multiply when you're working remotely. Is your upgraded internet connection a business expense if you use it for work? What about the ergonomic chair that helps you work more comfortably? The coffee you drink during video calls? The co-working space membership when your home gets too distracting? The line between personal and business expenses has gotten blurrier than a video call with bad connection.

Personal use of company resources is a gray area that most people navigate inconsistently. Everyone uses their work computer for some personal activities, but where's the line between checking personal email and running a side business? Most people understand that ordering personal items with the company account is wrong, but what about using company software licenses or office space for personal projects?

Home office boundaries create new integrity challenges. When your bedroom is your office, your kitchen table is your conference room, and your personal laptop doubles as your work computer, the separation between company resources and personal resources becomes meaningless. The electricity powering your computer, the internet connection enabling your video calls, and the space where you work are all personal resources being used for business purposes.

Time theft takes new forms in remote work environments. It's not just about leaving early or taking long lunches anymore. It's about claiming to be working while running errands, attending personal appointments during work hours without logging time off, or being "available" online while focused on personal tasks.

The compound effect of small compromises is dangerous because each individual decision seems minor, but the cumulative impact can be significant. The employee who occasionally rounds up their hours, sometimes uses company software for personal projects, and frequently stretches the definition of business expenses hasn't committed any major violations, but they've created a pattern that undermines trust.

Contractor loyalty presents unique ethical challenges when you're working for multiple clients simultaneously. How do you ensure that insights gained from one client don't inappropriately benefit another? How do you manage scheduling conflicts fairly? How do you handle requests that might put your different clients' interests in direct competition?

Investment conflicts become more complex as employees gain stock options, invest in index funds, or own cryptocurrency that might be affected by their work decisions. The software engineer whose retirement fund owns stock in companies that compete with their employer, the marketing manager who holds cryptocurrency that their company might adopt, the analyst who invests in companies they might be asked to evaluate all face potential conflicts.

Digital forensics mean that integrity violations leave traces that can be discovered months or years later. Email metadata, document version histories, file access logs, and browser histories create permanent records of actions that used to be ephemeral. The assumption that digital wrongdoing will go unnoticed is increasingly naive.

Outsourcing ethics get complicated when you're using platforms like Upwork or Fiverr to supplement your work capacity. If you hire a freelancer to help with a project, are you obligated to disclose that? What about using template services, stock photo sites, or pre-written code libraries? The line between legitimate resource usage and misrepresenting your own capabilities isn't always clear.

Side business boundaries require careful navigation when your employer's intellectual property, customer relationships, or competitive positioning might be affected. The consultant who starts their own firm, the employee who freelances in their spare time, or the manager who invests in startups all need to consider how their outside activities might create conflicts with their primary employment.

Modern integrity requires adapting timeless principles to new situations and technologies. The core values of honesty, fairness, and responsibility haven't changed, but the contexts in which we apply them have become more complex. Navigating these complexities requires thoughtful consideration of the principles involved and the likely consequences of different choices.

Integrity in the modern workplace isn't a single dramatic choice; it's the accumulation of hundreds of small ones that nobody is monitoring. The employee who doesn't inflate their hours when nobody would notice, who discloses the AI assistance on the proposal, who draws the line on the expense report even when the line is blurry — that pattern becomes their reputation. And reputation, as discussed in Chapter 2, compounds.

Case Study: GitHub's Government Contracts: When Employee Values Clash with Business Decisions

GitHub faced internal rebellion when employees learned the platform was being used by ICE (Immigration and Customs Enforcement) for activities they considered unethical. Employees organized protests, wrote open letters, and demanded the company cancel government contracts.

The situation forced GitHub to navigate competing obligations: contractual commitments to government customers, employee moral concerns, and their own stated values about open access to technology. Some employees felt complicit in policies they opposed; others argued that governments have legitimate needs for software tools.

GitHub ultimately kept the contracts but increased transparency about government partnerships and created channels for employee feedback on ethical concerns. The incident shows how individual integrity challenges become organizational problems when personal values conflict with business decisions.

Case Study: Signal's Privacy Principles

Signal's approach to encrypted messaging demonstrates how technology companies can prioritize user privacy over business growth and government pressure. The company's technical architecture makes it impossible for even Signal itself to access user communications.

Signal's integrity is demonstrated through its rejection of features that would compromise privacy, even when those features might increase user adoption or revenue. The company consistently chooses user protection over business optimization.

When governments pressure Signal to create backdoors or weaken encryption, the company refuses and explains publicly why compromises would fundamentally undermine user security. This transparency builds trust and educates users about privacy trade-offs.

Signal's funding model through donations instead of advertising or data sales aligns its business interests with user privacy. The company doesn't need to monetize user data because it doesn't depend on that revenue stream.

Case Study: Volkswagen's Emissions Fraud

Volkswagen's diesel emissions scandal shows how integrity failures can compound across an organization when competitive pressure overrides ethical constraints. The company programmed software to cheat on emissions tests while marketing their vehicles as environmentally friendly.

The fraud wasn't the result of individual bad actors but systematic corporate decisions to prioritize market performance over environmental regulations and customer honesty. Engineers, managers, and executives all participated in maintaining the deception.

The scandal affected millions of vehicles worldwide and contributed to air pollution that harmed public health. Volkswagen's deception had real environmental and health consequences beyond just regulatory violations.

The company's eventual admission of guilt and massive financial penalties showed that integrity violations eventually become more expensive than honest compliance would have been. The short-term competitive advantages were overwhelmed by long-term costs.

Chapter 10: Work-Life Integration

Work-life balance used to mean leaving the office at 5 PM and not thinking about work until 9 AM the next day. Now it means trying to maintain some semblance of personal identity while your kitchen table serves as your conference room, your bedroom wall is your video call background, and your cat has become a regular participant in client meetings.

The phrase "work-life balance" has become almost quaint in a world where the boundaries between work and life have been obliterated by technology and remote work. We've moved from balance to integration, which sounds nicer but mostly means that work has invaded every corner of your personal space and most hours of your day.

Family and personal life in home offices create complications that office workers never had to consider. Your children might interrupt important calls, your partner might need the space you're using for work, or your neighbors might start construction projects during your most important meetings. These aren't just logistical challenges; they're ethical dilemmas about professionalism and accommodation.

Childcare during work hours has become a reality for many remote workers, especially during school closures or when regular childcare arrangements fall through. The ethics of childcare during work involve being honest about your availability while still meeting your professional obligations. It's not fair to your colleagues or clients to pretend you're fully focused when you're managing a toddler's meltdown.

The guilt associated with working from home comes from multiple directions. You might feel guilty about not being fully present for family when you're working in shared spaces, guilty about not being fully focused on work when family needs interrupt, or guilty about the advantages you have compared to colleagues who struggle with home office setups.

Domestic partnership challenges multiply when both partners are working from home in limited space. Who gets the quiet room for important calls? How do you coordinate schedules when you both have back-to-back meetings? How do you maintain professional boundaries when your partner can hear every conversation you have with colleagues? These questions require ongoing negotiation and compromise that can strain even strong relationships.

Personal relationships suffer when work expands to fill all available time and space. It's harder to be fully present with family and friends when your work email is always within reach and your mind is constantly processing professional concerns. The relationships that used to provide refuge from work stress now compete with work for attention and energy.

Children's understanding of work becomes complicated when they see you at home but can't interact with you because you're "working." The concept of being physically present but professionally unavailable is confusing for kids, and the constant need to explain why they can't talk to you right now can create tension and resentment.

Social isolation affects even people who were comfortable working alone before remote work became widespread. The casual interactions that used to provide social connection throughout the day disappear when you're working from home full-time. Conversations with colleagues, interactions with service workers, chance encounters with neighbors all vanish when your world shrinks to your living space.

Exercise and physical health become more challenging when your commute is eliminated and your workplace is sedentary. The walking that used to happen naturally throughout the workday disappears when everything you need is within arm's reach. Maintaining physical health requires more intentional effort and planning when your work environment is also your living environment.

Personal space invasion happens gradually and then suddenly. It starts with checking email after dinner, progresses to taking calls during family time, and eventually reaches the point where you're never fully off work because work has colonized your entire living space. Reclaiming personal space requires intentional effort and sometimes physical changes to your environment.

Community connection suffers when your daily routine doesn't include natural opportunities for social interaction. The neighbors you used to see during your commute, the coffee shop workers who knew your order, the colleagues you'd chat with in hallways all disappear when you're working from home. Building community requires more deliberate effort.

Personal identity can become subsumed by professional identity when work takes over your living space and most of your waking hours. The hobbies, relationships, and activities that used to define who you are outside of work can fade when there's no clear separation between work time and personal time.

Financial boundaries get complicated when your home becomes your office. Which utility costs are business expenses? How do you separate personal and professional use of your internet connection? What about furniture, equipment, or software that serves dual purposes? The tax implications and ethical considerations of home office expenses require careful consideration.

Household maintenance becomes a source of conflict when one person is working from home and the other isn't. The person at home might be expected to handle deliveries, repair appointments, or cleaning, even though they're theoretically working. These expectations can create resentment and blur the lines between being home and being available for household tasks.

Privacy within relationships gets complicated when your partner can overhear confidential work conversations or see sensitive information on your screen. Maintaining professional confidentiality while sharing living space requires physical arrangements and agreements that many couples haven't had to navigate before.

Eldercare responsibilities often fall disproportionately on remote workers because they're "home anyway." The assumption that being physically present means being available for caregiving responsibilities can create impossible conflicts between professional obligations and family needs.

The comparison trap is dangerous in remote work environments where you only see curated glimpses of other people's work setups through video calls and social media. The colleague with the perfect home office, the friend who seems to effortlessly balance work and family, or the influencer who makes remote work look glamorous can create unrealistic expectations and feelings of inadequacy.

Recovery time becomes crucial but harder to achieve when your work environment is always present. The psychological transition from work mode to personal mode used to happen during commutes or when you physically left the office. Now you have to create these transitions artificially, and many people skip them entirely.

The ethics of work-life integration come down to protecting your humanity while meeting your professional obligations. This means setting boundaries that preserve your health, relationships, and personal identity, even when those boundaries are inconvenient for work. It means being honest about your limitations and needs while still being reliable and professional.

Work-life integration is about creating sustainable patterns that allow you to be effective professionally without sacrificing your wellbeing personally. This requires ongoing attention and adjustment as circumstances change, and it requires the recognition that perfect balance is impossible but thoughtful integration is achievable.

Case Study: Automattic's Distributed Workforce: Redefining Work-Life Boundaries

Automattic, the company behind WordPress, operates as a fully distributed company with employees in over 90 countries. Their approach to work-life integration provides insights into both the opportunities and challenges of location-independent work.

Employees have complete flexibility over when and where they work, but they also face the challenge of creating boundaries when work can happen anywhere, anytime. The company provides co-working allowances and encourages regular "meetups," but many employees struggle with isolation and overwork.

Automattic's experience shows that flexibility alone doesn't solve work-life integration challenges. Without intentional boundary-setting, unlimited flexibility can become unlimited availability. Their model demonstrates both the promise and the pitfalls of trying to eliminate traditional work constraints.

Case Study: Shopify's Support for Distributed Families

Shopify's approach to supporting employees with distributed families shows how companies can address work-life integration challenges thoughtfully. The company provides stipends for family visits, flexible schedules for international time zones, and support for employees who want to work near aging parents or extended family.

The company recognizes that employees' personal obligations don't disappear just because they work remotely, and they've created policies that accommodate family responsibilities instead of ignoring them. This approach reduces stress and increases loyalty.

Shopify's family support policies are applied consistently regardless of family structure, recognizing that different employees have different caregiving responsibilities. The flexibility helps everyone integrate work and personal life more effectively.

The company measures employee satisfaction and retention as indicators of whether their work-life integration policies are helping people instead of just creating good publicity.

Case Study: Goldman Sachs' Junior Analyst Burnout

Goldman Sachs faced criticism when junior analysts created a presentation detailing the unsustainable working conditions they faced, including 100-hour work weeks and severe impacts on their physical and mental health.

The analysts' presentation showed how financial firms' culture of extreme hours creates ethical problems when young employees feel they must sacrifice their health for career advancement. The competitive environment makes it difficult for people to set boundaries without hurting their prospects.

The firm's initial response focused on cosmetic changes like protected Saturdays instead of addressing the underlying culture that rewards overwork and treats burnout as a sign of weakness instead of poor management.

The incident highlighted how industries with extreme work cultures create ethical dilemmas for both employees and employers about sustainable career development and human welfare.

Chapter 11: Diversity, Equity, and Inclusion

Diversity, equity, and inclusion have gone from nice-to-have corporate initiatives to mandatory training sessions that everyone endures while secretly checking their phones. The challenge isn't that DEI principles are wrong (they're not), but that implementation often feels disconnected from the experience of working with diverse groups of people.

The ethics of DEI start with understanding what genuine inclusion looks like in practice. Real inclusion requires changing systems, processes, and cultures, not just changing demographics. It's about creating environments where people from different backgrounds can contribute their best work and advance based on their capabilities.

Allyship and advocacy require more than expressing support for diversity on social media or attending voluntary training sessions. Real allyship means using your privilege and influence to create opportunities for others, speaking up when you witness exclusionary behavior, and amplifying voices that might not otherwise be heard. It also means recognizing when to step back and let others lead.

The practical aspects of allyship often involve small, daily actions that compound. Recommending colleagues for speaking opportunities, making sure credit gets distributed fairly in meetings, asking whose voices are missing from important conversations, and creating space for different perspectives all contribute to more inclusive environments.

Intersectionality means recognizing that people's identities are complex and that someone might face different challenges based on multiple aspects of who they are. A Black woman's experience in the workplace isn't just the sum of being Black plus being a woman; it's a unique experience that combines both identities in ways that create challenges and perspectives.

Intersectionality, once understood, helps avoid oversimplified approaches to inclusion that treat identity categories as monolithic. The strategies that work for supporting women might not work for supporting women of color. The accommodations that help people with disabilities might need to be different for people who also face other forms of discrimination.

Cultural competence becomes important as workplaces become more diverse, but it can't be reduced to learning lists of do's and don'ts for different cultures. Real cultural competence means developing the skills to work effectively with people who have different communication styles, values, and approaches to work relationships. It's about flexibility and empathy, not memorizing cultural facts.

Cultural competence involves recognizing your own cultural assumptions and understanding how they affect your interactions with others. The communication style that feels natural to you might be uncomfortable for someone from a different background. The way you prefer to receive feedback might not work for everyone on your team.

Disability inclusion is often overlooked in DEI conversations, but it affects more people than most organizations realize. Creating accessible workplaces isn't just about wheelchair ramps and screen readers; it's about flexible work arrangements, clear communication, and recognizing that people have different needs and capabilities.

The principles of universal design benefit everyone, not just people with diagnosed disabilities. Captions on videos help people with hearing impairments, but they also help people working in noisy environments or whose first language isn't English. Clear, simple communication helps people with cognitive differences, but it also helps everyone understand information more quickly.

Generational diversity creates its own challenges as workplaces span people with vastly different experiences of technology, communication, and professional norms. What seems like common sense to a digital native might be foreign to someone who started their career before email existed, and vice versa.

Managing generational differences requires avoiding stereotypes while acknowledging real differences in experience and preference. Not every older worker struggles with technology, and not every younger worker prefers informal communication. The key is creating systems that work for different styles and preferences instead of assuming everyone should adapt to one approach.

Inclusive hiring practices go beyond posting jobs in diverse places or removing identifying information from resumes. They involve examining whether your job requirements are necessary, whether your interview process favors certain communication styles, and whether your company culture would be welcoming to people from different backgrounds.

Rethinking qualifications often reveals that many job requirements aren't essential and may exclude qualified candidates unnecessarily. Requiring college degrees for positions that don't need them, demanding years of experience instead of demonstrated competencies, or insisting on technical skills that could be learned on the job all create barriers that disproportionately affect certain groups.

Pay equity requires more than ensuring people in identical roles receive identical compensation. It means examining whether women and people of color are clustered in lower-paying roles, whether promotion patterns create wage gaps, and whether "soft skills" that affect compensation are evaluated fairly across different groups.

Addressing pay gaps requires understanding how they develop. They might start with hiring decisions, grow through promotion processes, or expand through performance evaluation systems that favor certain communication styles or cultural approaches to self-advocacy.

The emotional labor of DEI work often falls disproportionately on people from underrepresented groups, who are expected to educate their colleagues, serve on diversity committees, and provide perspectives on inclusion initiatives in addition to their regular job responsibilities. This additional burden should be recognized and compensated appropriately.

Distributing DEI responsibilities more fairly means involving people from majority groups in inclusion work and ensuring that diversity initiatives don't become additional unpaid work for the people they're intended to help. Everyone benefits from inclusive workplaces, so everyone should contribute to creating them.

Mentorship and sponsorship programs can help address systemic barriers to advancement, but they need to be structured thoughtfully to avoid creating additional burdens or reinforcing existing inequities. Effective programs provide clear expectations, adequate training, and meaningful support for both mentors and mentees.

The difference between mentorship and sponsorship is crucial. Mentors provide advice and guidance. Sponsors use their influence to create opportunities and advocate for advancement. Both are valuable, but sponsorship is often more important for breaking through barriers to senior positions.

Employee resource groups can provide valuable support and community for people from similar backgrounds, but they work best when they're supported by leadership and integrated into broader inclusion efforts. ERGs shouldn't be expected to solve diversity problems on their own or to represent the views of entire demographic groups.

Measuring progress in DEI requires both quantitative and qualitative metrics. Numbers tell you about representation, but they don't tell you about belonging, advancement opportunities, or day-to-day experiences. Exit interviews, engagement surveys, and informal feedback can provide insights that demographic data can't capture.

Effective measurement involves tracking outcomes instead of just inputs. It's not enough to know how many diverse candidates you interviewed; you need to know how many were hired, how they performed, whether they were promoted, and whether they stayed with the organization.

Sustainable DEI work requires commitment and systems thinking instead of quick fixes or one-time initiatives. It means examining policies, practices, and cultures systematically and making changes that will persist even when leadership changes or priorities shift.

Sustainable inclusion means embedding equity considerations into regular business processes instead of treating diversity as a separate initiative. When inclusion becomes part of how you hire, promote, evaluate performance, and make decisions, it's more likely to persist and create lasting change.

The ethics of DEI come down to treating people fairly while recognizing that fairness sometimes requires different treatment. It's about creating environments where everyone can contribute their best work and advance based on their capabilities and effort. Most importantly, it's about recognizing that inclusion benefits everyone, not just people from underrepresented groups.

Case Study: Salesforce's Equal Pay Initiative: Proactive DEI in Practice

When Salesforce discovered gender pay gaps through internal audits, they didn't wait for complaints or lawsuits. CEO Marc Benioff committed to spending millions of dollars to eliminate pay disparities and conduct ongoing assessments to prevent future gaps.

The initiative required examining not just individual salaries but the systemic factors that created disparities: promotion patterns, performance evaluation criteria, and job classification systems. Salesforce found that equal pay required more than equal starting salaries; it required equal advancement opportunities.

Their approach demonstrates how effective DEI work requires ongoing commitment and resources, not just one-time fixes. By being proactive instead of reactive, Salesforce turned a potential liability into a competitive advantage for recruiting and retention.

Case Study: Accenture's Systematic DEI Approach

Accenture's diversity efforts demonstrate how large organizations can make meaningful progress on inclusion through systematic measurement and accountability. The company has achieved gender parity globally and continues to work on racial and ethnic diversity.

The company's approach works because it ties diversity metrics to executive compensation and business strategy instead of treating inclusion as a separate HR initiative. Leaders know their advancement depends partly on creating inclusive teams and developing diverse talent.

Accenture's focus on inclusive leadership development helps managers understand how bias affects decision-making and how to create environments where diverse teams can succeed. This skills-based approach is more effective than awareness training alone.

The company's transparency about diversity data and progress creates accountability and allows other organizations to learn from their successes and failures. This openness advances industry-wide progress instead of just internal improvement.

Case Study: Google's AI Ethics Team Dissolution

Google's handling of its AI ethics team shows how corporate DEI commitments can conflict with business interests when ethical concerns threaten profitable projects. The company fired prominent ethics researchers who raised concerns about AI bias and environmental impact.

Timnit Gebru and Margaret Mitchell's research on AI language models challenged Google's business strategy by highlighting how these systems can perpetuate discrimination and consume enormous environmental resources. Their firing suggested that diversity and inclusion were valued only when they didn't threaten core business interests.

The firings damaged Google's credibility on AI ethics and DEI issues because they showed that the company wasn't willing to support diverse voices when they raised inconvenient truths about business practices.

The incident illustrated how technology companies can use DEI initiatives as public relations tools while suppressing internal voices that challenge profitable but problematic business practices.

Chapter 12: When DEI Becomes Unethical

Diversity, equity, and inclusion initiatives can sometimes become the very thing they're supposed to prevent: unfair, discriminatory, and divisive. This isn't an argument against DEI principles, which are fundamentally sound, but a recognition that good intentions can lead to bad outcomes when implementation goes wrong or when the pursuit of equity crosses the line into creating new forms of injustice.

Overcorrection happens when organizations swing so far toward inclusion that they create new forms of exclusion. The company that becomes so focused on hiring from underrepresented groups that they stop considering qualified candidates from majority backgrounds, the university that prioritizes diversity over academic preparation, or the organization that assumes all members of certain groups need extra support regardless of their individual circumstances.

The pendulum effect creates situations where yesterday's disadvantaged groups become today's excluded ones. White men in their twenties who can't find entry-level positions because every program is targeted at other demographics, experienced employees who get passed over for leadership development because they don't fit current diversity priorities, or qualified candidates who never get interviewed because their demographics don't match organizational goals.

Ideological conformity sometimes becomes an unspoken requirement in organizations with strong DEI commitments. Employees who have questions about diversity initiatives, who don't enthusiastically participate in inclusion activities, or who express concerns about implementation approaches can face social and professional consequences for not demonstrating sufficient commitment to the cause.

A culture of ideological surveillance emerges when organizations monitor employees' social media for unapproved viewpoints, when expressing certain opinions becomes grounds for discipline or termination, or when people feel they have to hide their political beliefs, religious views, or cultural backgrounds to avoid being labeled as problematic.

Diversity loyalty tests put employees in impossible positions where they're expected to publicly support initiatives they might privately question, participate in activities that conflict with their personal values, or express enthusiasm for policies they think are poorly designed. Silence becomes suspicious, and dissent becomes dangerous.

Victim hierarchy emerges when organizations prioritize certain types of diversity over others or when different groups compete for attention and resources. The focus on racial diversity that ignores socioeconomic background, the emphasis on gender equality that excludes men from support programs, or the attention to sexual orientation that overlooks religious diversity all create situations where some inclusion comes at the expense of others.

These hierarchies can pit underrepresented groups against each other instead of addressing systemic barriers that affect everyone. When diversity becomes a zero-sum competition for limited resources and attention, it undermines the coalition-building that effective inclusion requires. The Black employee and the Hispanic employee competing for the same diversity scholarship, the women's network and the LGBTQ group fighting over the same budget allocation.

Cultural imperialism can emerge when DEI initiatives impose dominant cultural values under the guise of inclusion. The assumption that everyone should embrace identical definitions of success, communication styles, or workplace relationships can erase cultural differences instead of celebrating them. True inclusion requires accommodating different values and approaches, not converting everyone to a single worldview.

DEI programs that assume a specific political or ideological framework can alienate employees whose values or cultural backgrounds differ from those assumptions — including people with traditional religious beliefs, conservative viewpoints, or cultures that emphasize hierarchy, family obligation, or personal responsibility. When inclusion becomes synonymous with a particular worldview rather than a practical commitment to fairness, it excludes people who support diversity but approach it differently.

When DEI becomes a moral crusade that demands ideological conversion rather than a practical strategy that requires implementation, it creates unnecessary conflict and resistance among people who might otherwise support diversity goals. Inclusion works better as a set of policies and practices than as a test of moral character.

Mandatory allyship programs that require employees to publicly enumerate their privilege, denounce their advantages, or commit to specific political positions cross the line from education into indoctrination. People who support equal opportunity but resist being forced to adopt particular worldviews or express beliefs end up being labeled as resistant or problematic.

Equity theater substitutes dramatic gestures for substantive change while creating spectacles that make everyone uncomfortable. The land acknowledgments that serve no practical purpose, the privilege walks that shame participants, or the mandatory bias confessions that force people to admit to prejudices they may not hold all create performative displays instead of genuine progress.

These theatrical approaches often generate more heat than light, creating resentment among participants while failing to address the practical barriers that prevent inclusion. They're designed more to demonstrate ideological purity than to solve real problems.

Identity essentialism treats people as representatives of their demographic groups instead of as people with unique perspectives and experiences. The assumption that all women think alike, that people of the same race share identical viewpoints, or that sexual orientation determines political beliefs reduces complex human beings to simple categories.

This essentialism creates impossible expectations for people from underrepresented groups who are expected to think, act, and believe in ways that conform to organizational assumptions about their identities. The conservative Black employee, the traditional Muslim woman, or the libertarian gay man all face pressure to conform to stereotypes about how people like them should think and behave.

Backlash management requires acknowledging that some resistance to DEI initiatives comes from legitimate concerns about fairness, implementation, or ideological pressure instead of from prejudice or ignorance. People who feel blamed for problems they didn't create, excluded from solutions they don't understand, or pressured to embrace viewpoints they don't share will resist diversity efforts regardless of their merit.

Dismissing all criticism of DEI implementation as racism, sexism, or bias prevents organizations from learning from mistakes and improving their approaches. Some people who express concerns about diversity initiatives are genuinely committed to fairness but have different ideas about how to achieve it.

The accountability gap emerges when organizations hold some groups to higher standards than others, excuse poor performance from preferred demographics, or fail to address problems when they come from people in protected categories. Equal treatment means equal expectations and equal consequences, not different standards for different groups.

When DEI becomes unethical, it's usually because it's been implemented as an ideological program instead of a practical business strategy. The solution isn't to abandon efforts toward inclusion, but to pursue them with more nuance, fairness, and attention to unintended consequences.

Sustainable diversity requires building broad coalitions instead of narrow constituencies. When inclusion efforts benefit only groups or when they're perceived as zero-sum competitions, they create division instead of unity. The most effective DEI initiatives expand opportunity for everyone while paying attention to barriers that affect underrepresented groups.

The goal should be creating workplaces where people are evaluated based on their capabilities and character instead of their demographics, where everyone has equal opportunities to succeed regardless of their background, and where different perspectives are valued without requiring conformity to particular political or ideological positions.

Good intentions aren't enough; good outcomes require good implementation that respects individual dignity, maintains fairness for everyone, and focuses on practical solutions instead of ideological purity. When DEI serves people instead of requiring people to serve DEI, it achieves its intended purpose of creating more inclusive and effective organizations.

Case Study: Gig Workers at Uber and Lyft: Redefining Employment Ethics

The classification of Uber and Lyft drivers as independent contractors instead of employees has created new ethical challenges about worker rights, benefits, and platform responsibility. Drivers bear the costs and risks of vehicle ownership and maintenance while platforms control pricing, routing, and customer access.

California's AB5 law attempted to reclassify gig workers as employees, but Uber and Lyft spent over $200 million on a ballot initiative (Proposition 22) to maintain contractor status while providing limited benefits. The campaign raised questions about corporate influence on labor law and worker representation.

This ongoing battle illustrates how technological innovation can outpace regulatory frameworks, creating gray areas where traditional employment protections don't apply. It shows how emerging business models can shift economic risks from companies to workers without clear ethical guidelines.

Case Study: Patreon's Creator Economy Policies

Patreon's approach to platform governance shows how companies can balance creator freedom with content responsibility. The platform has developed sophisticated policies for handling controversial content while supporting diverse creators financially.

The company's challenge is creating rules that protect users from harassment and illegal content while avoiding censorship that could damage creators' livelihoods. Their approach emphasizes transparency about policy decisions and appeals processes for disputed actions.

Patreon's creator-focused business model aligns its interests with creator success instead of just engagement metrics. This alignment encourages policies that support sustainable creative careers instead of maximizing short-term attention.

The platform's willingness to lose controversial creators instead of compromise safety policies shows how companies can prioritize ethical considerations over revenue when their values are clear and consistently applied.

Case Study: DoorDash's Gig Worker Classification

DoorDash's treatment of delivery drivers illustrates the ethical complexities of gig economy employment. The company classifies drivers as independent contractors while controlling many aspects of their work experience through algorithmic management.

The classification affects drivers' access to benefits, job protections, and income stability. DoorDash's policies shift economic risks from the company to individual workers while maintaining control over pricing, routing, and customer relationships.

The company's response to regulation attempts shows how gig economy companies use political influence to maintain favorable employment classifications instead of accepting higher labor costs or different business models.

The debate over driver classification reflects broader questions about how employment relationships should adapt to technological change and whether traditional worker protections should apply to platform-mediated work.

Chapter 13: Emerging Challenges

The workplace is evolving faster than a software update you didn't ask for, and just when you think you've figured out the rules, someone invents a new technology that makes half of them obsolete. We're dealing with ethical challenges that would have been science fiction a decade ago, and we're making up the rules as we go along.

Gig economy relationships have created a new category of worker that doesn't fit neatly into traditional employment frameworks. Independent contractors who work full-time for single clients, freelancers who depend on platform algorithms for income, and consultants who blur the line between employee and vendor all face ethical challenges that didn't exist in simpler employment models.

The ethics of gig work include questions about benefits, job security, and workplace protections. Should companies that rely heavily on contractors provide health insurance or retirement benefits? What obligations do platforms have to workers whose livelihoods depend on algorithmic decisions they can't control or appeal? How do you create career development opportunities for people who technically aren't employees?

Platform dependency creates power imbalances that can be exploitative even when they're technically voluntary. When your income depends on maintaining good ratings on a platform you don't control, when algorithm changes can eliminate your visibility overnight, or when platform policies can change without notice, you're vulnerable in ways that traditional employees aren't.

The ethics of algorithmic management affect millions of workers whose schedules, pay, and job security depend on automated systems. Delivery drivers whose routes are optimized by algorithms, freelancers whose project visibility depends on platform rankings, and remote workers whose productivity is monitored by software all face challenges that human managers might handle with discretion but algorithms handle with rigid logic.

These systems often embed biases that their creators never intended. An algorithm that optimizes for efficiency might systematically disadvantage workers with disabilities. A ranking system that rewards quick responses might favor workers in certain time zones or with home office setups. The opacity of these systems makes it hard for workers to understand why they're being treated unfairly, let alone appeal the decisions.

Environmental responsibility in business operations has become unavoidable as climate change affects everything from supply chains to office locations. The carbon footprint of digital infrastructure, the environmental impact of product packaging, and the sustainability of vendor relationships all create ethical obligations that previous generations of workers didn't have to consider.

Corporate environmental responsibility creates individual ethical dilemmas when personal values conflict with business practices. The employee who believes in environmental protection but works for a company with poor sustainability practices faces daily compromises. The manager who wants to reduce travel but faces pressure to maintain client relationships through in-person meetings has to balance competing obligations.

Supply chain ethics have become more visible and complex as global trade networks reveal their hidden costs. The smartphone you use for work, the clothes you wear to meetings, and the coffee you drink during conference calls all have supply chains that might involve labor exploitation, environmental damage, or human rights violations.

The challenge with supply chain responsibility is that individual consumers and employees have limited information and influence over these complex systems. You can make personal choices about what products to buy and what companies to work for, but systemic problems require collective action and regulatory changes that go beyond individual ethics.

Cybersecurity has become everyone's responsibility, not just the IT department's. The passwords you choose, the networks you connect to, and the emails you open all affect organizational security. But individual security practices have to be balanced against usability and productivity.

The ethics of cybersecurity include questions about monitoring, privacy, and shared responsibility. How much inconvenience should employees accept in the name of security? What information should organizations collect about employee online activities? How do you balance security requirements with privacy expectations and productivity needs?

Security theater can be as problematic as inadequate security. Policies that create the appearance of protection without benefits waste time and resources while creating false confidence. The monthly password changes that encourage weak passwords, the email warnings that train people to ignore security alerts, and the access restrictions that drive people to find workarounds all undermine real security.

Data sovereignty and privacy have become workplace issues as organizations collect, store, and analyze unprecedented amounts of information about employees, customers, and business operations. The data you generate through your work, the information you access about others, and the digital trails you create all have privacy and security implications.

Cross-border data transfer creates legal and ethical complications when information about European employees gets stored on US servers, when customer data gets processed in countries with different privacy laws, or when government requests for information conflict with privacy obligations.

The ethics of data collection include questions about consent, purpose limitation, and retention. Just because technology makes it possible to collect detailed information about employee productivity, customer behavior, or business operations doesn't mean it's ethical to do so. The principle of data minimization suggests collecting only what's necessary for legitimate business purposes.

Generational wealth gaps affect workplace relationships in ways that aren't always visible. Colleagues with family financial support can take risks, accept lower-paying opportunities, or work unpaid internships that aren't available to people without financial safety nets. These advantages compound and affect career trajectories in ways that aren't related to talent or effort.

The ethics of advantage recognition include acknowledging how privilege affects opportunities while avoiding guilt or resentment that doesn't help anyone. Understanding why some colleagues can afford to take career risks that others can't helps explain outcome differences without justifying unfairness.

Unpaid internships and "portfolio careers" often require financial support that not everyone has access to. The expectation that people will work for free to gain experience, accept below-market rates to build portfolios, or invest in expensive training and certification programs creates barriers that favor people with existing wealth.

Cryptocurrency and digital assets — now firmly part of the financial mainstream rather than a speculative fringe — have created new forms of conflict of interest that most organizations are still figuring out how to govern. Employees who invest in digital currencies or work at companies building on blockchain infrastructure may face situations where their personal holdings intersect with employer decisions in ways traditional conflict-of-interest policies weren't written to handle. The volatility of digital assets compounds the challenge: an employee whose crypto holdings spike during a period when their employer is evaluating a blockchain partnership faces a genuine ethical question about objectivity that existing equity-based conflict-of-interest frameworks don't map onto cleanly.

Biometric data collection in workplaces raises privacy and security concerns that go beyond traditional background checks or drug testing. Fingerprint scanners, facial recognition systems, and health monitoring devices collect information that's impossible to change if it's compromised and difficult to separate from personal identity.

The ethics of biometric workplace surveillance include questions about consent, necessity, and proportionality. Is fingerprint access control justified for routine office buildings? Should employers be able to monitor employee health data for safety purposes? How do you balance legitimate security needs with privacy rights?

Virtual and augmented reality technologies have moved well beyond novelty into real workplace deployment, and the ethical challenges they create are no longer theoretical. VR training programs, AR-assisted maintenance procedures, and virtual collaboration environments all blur the lines between physical and digital experience in ways that affect privacy, safety, and workplace relationships.

The immersive nature of these technologies creates unique risks for harassment, manipulation, and psychological harm. The colleague who behaves inappropriately in virtual reality, the training program that creates unrealistic stress or trauma, or the AR system that affects perception and judgment all create liability and ethical questions that existing frameworks don't address well.

Emerging challenges require adapting ethical frameworks to new situations while maintaining core principles of fairness, honesty, and respect. The technologies and social changes will continue evolving, but the fundamental questions about how we treat each other and share resources remain constant.

The goal isn't to predict every future challenge or create rules for situations that haven't happened yet. The goal is to develop the ethical judgment and flexibility to navigate new situations thoughtfully while staying grounded in principles that promote human flourishing and social cooperation.

Case Study: Working for Adam Neumann at WeWork: Charismatic Leadership Gone Wrong

Adam Neumann's leadership of WeWork provides a case study in how charismatic but unethical bosses can create unsustainable work environments. Employees described a culture of excessive drinking, bizarre decision-making, and financial irresponsibility masked by inspirational rhetoric about "elevating consciousness."

Neumann's behavior included conflicts of interest (leasing buildings he owned to WeWork), questionable expenses (private jets, expensive alcohol), and erratic management decisions that affected thousands of employees. Many employees knew the situation was unsustainable but felt trapped by golden handcuffs and the cult-like atmosphere Neumann created.

The company's failed IPO and Neumann's eventual ouster demonstrate how unethical leadership eventually catches up with even the most successful-seeming organizations. Employees who spoke up early were vindicated, while those who stayed silent watched their equity become worthless.

Case Study: Safra Catz's Oracle Leadership

Oracle CEO Safra Catz's leadership style demonstrates how executives can maintain high performance standards while treating employees fairly. Her approach shows that demanding excellence doesn't require creating toxic work environments or using fear-based management.

Catz's focus on operational efficiency and financial discipline creates clear expectations for performance while providing employees with the resources and support they need to succeed. This combination of high standards and adequate support prevents the impossible situations that characterize toxic leadership.

The company's retention of top talent under Catz's leadership suggests that people can thrive under demanding but fair leadership when they know what's expected and have the tools to deliver results.

Oracle's business success under Catz's leadership shows that ethical management practices can coexist with aggressive business strategy when leaders distinguish between competitive behavior toward rivals and treatment of their own employees.

Case Study: Elizabeth Holmes' Employee Manipulation

Elizabeth Holmes' management of Theranos employees shows how charismatic but unethical leaders can exploit people's good intentions and professional aspirations. Her approach combined inspiration with intimidation to maintain loyalty despite obvious problems.

Holmes created a culture of secrecy and paranoia where employees were afraid to share information with each other or ask questions about the technology they were supposedly developing. This isolation prevented people from recognizing the scope of the deception.

The company's legal agreements included extreme non-disclosure and non-compete clauses that made it financially dangerous for employees to leave or speak out about problems. These agreements trapped people in situations they knew were wrong.

Holmes' personal charm and compelling vision allowed her to recruit talented people who genuinely wanted to improve healthcare, then exploited their commitment to maintain a fraudulent organization.

Chapter 14: When the Boss is Not Ethical

Working for an unethical boss is like being trapped in a psychological thriller where you're never quite sure if you're the protagonist or just a disposable character. The good news is that you're not going crazy; the bad news is that your boss probably is making your work life a nightmare, and traditional HR advice about "having a conversation" is about as useful as a chocolate teapot.

The fundamental challenge with unethical bosses is the power imbalance. Unlike problematic colleagues who you can avoid or work around, your boss controls your assignments, evaluations, advancement opportunities, and potentially your employment. This power dynamic makes it much harder to address problems directly or escape the situation quickly.

Unethical leadership can be hard to recognize because toxic bosses are often skilled at making their behavior seem normal, necessary, or even beneficial. They're masters at gaslighting, blame-shifting, and creating environments where questioning their decisions feels dangerous or disloyal. The first step is trusting your instincts when something feels consistently wrong.

The credit thief boss presents your work as their own in meetings with senior leadership, takes ownership of successful projects while distancing themselves from failures, and somehow always manages to be the hero of every story they tell about team accomplishments. They've perfected the art of making your contributions disappear while amplifying their own role.

The micromanager boss demands constant updates while providing no clear direction, requires approval for decisions you're qualified to make independently, and somehow finds time to nitpick your work while being unavailable when you need guidance. They create dependency while complaining about your lack of initiative.

The favoritism boss rewards loyalty over competence, gives the best assignments to their personal favorites regardless of qualifications, and creates an inner circle of trusted employees who get better treatment, information, and opportunities. Merit becomes secondary to personal relationships and political allegiance.

The scapegoat boss takes credit for successes but disappears when things go wrong, blames their team for problems they created through poor decisions or inadequate resources, and has perfected the art of upward accountability while showing no downward responsibility. They're Teflon-coated when it comes to consequences.

Managing up becomes perverse when your boss is unethical. Traditional advice about understanding your boss's goals and helping them succeed doesn't work when their goals are problematic or their success comes at your expense. Instead, you have to focus on protecting yourself while appearing cooperative.

The information control strategy is common among unethical bosses who limit your access to senior leadership, filter communications so you only hear their version of events, prevent you from building independent relationships within the organization, and make you dependent on them for context about organizational decisions and priorities.

Working around unethical leadership requires developing alternative sources of information, building relationships with peers in other departments, finding ways to demonstrate your value to people outside your direct reporting line, and creating visibility for your work that doesn't depend entirely on your boss's advocacy.

The impossible standards trap involves bosses who set contradictory expectations, change requirements without notice, criticize you for decisions they previously approved, and create no-win situations where any choice you make can be used against you later. They maintain control by ensuring you can never fully succeed.

Protecting your reputation while working for an unethical boss requires strategic thinking about how your association with them affects your standing in the organization. You need to distance yourself from their questionable decisions while maintaining working relationships and avoiding the appearance of disloyalty.

The loyalty test is something many unethical bosses use to identify potential threats to their position. They might ask you to do something questionable to see if you'll comply, share confidential information to test your discretion, or ask for your opinion about other leaders to gauge your loyalty. These tests are designed to compromise you or gather information they can use later.

Psychological manipulation tactics include gaslighting you about events you clearly remember differently, alternating between praise and criticism to keep you off-balance, using personal information against you in professional contexts, and creating artificial urgency or crisis to justify unreasonable demands.

The isolation effect happens when unethical bosses systematically damage your relationships with colleagues, exclude you from important meetings or decisions, limit your access to training or development opportunities, and make you feel like you're the problem when their behavior is clearly inappropriate.

Career stagnation under unethical leadership occurs when bosses block your advancement opportunities, fail to advocate for your promotion or salary increases, prevent you from taking on challenging assignments that would develop your skills, and generally keep you trapped in your current role to maintain their control.

The complicity trap involves bosses who gradually involve you in questionable activities, start with small requests that seem harmless, then escalate to more problematic behavior, making you feel like you're equally responsible for problems they created. They're experts at distributing blame while maintaining deniability.

Boundary setting with unethical bosses is more complex than with peers because direct confrontation can result in retaliation. You have to find ways to protect your integrity without appearing insubordinate, which often means being creative about how you respond to problematic requests.

The transfer strategy works best in large organizations where you can move to different departments or locations. But unethical bosses often try to sabotage transfer attempts by providing poor references, blocking your applications, or spreading negative information about your performance to other managers.

Exit timing becomes crucial when you decide the situation is unsalvageable. Leaving too quickly might damage your financial security or career trajectory, but staying too long can affect your mental health and professional reputation. The key is planning your departure strategically while documenting any behavior that might affect your references.

Industry reputation management requires thinking about how your experience with an unethical boss might affect your standing in your professional community. If your boss is known for problematic behavior, people might understand your situation. If they have a good external reputation, you might need to be more careful about how you frame your experience.

The recovery process after working for an unethical boss can take time. Toxic leadership affects your confidence, judgment, and ability to trust future managers. Learning to recognize healthy leadership styles and rebuilding your professional self-esteem requires conscious effort and sometimes professional support.

Future prevention involves developing better interview skills for assessing potential bosses, asking strategic questions about management style and company culture, building stronger professional networks that can provide insights about potential employers, and recognizing warning signs early in new relationships.

When the boss is not ethical, your primary responsibility is to yourself and your family. You can't fix your boss, and you're not obligated to sacrifice your career, health, or wellbeing trying to reform someone who doesn't want to change. Sometimes the most ethical thing you can do is protect yourself and find a better situation where you can do meaningful work under competent leadership.

Case Study: Coca-Cola's "Be Less White" Training: When Inclusion Efforts Backfire

Coca-Cola faced backlash when screenshots of employee training materials instructing workers to "be less white" went viral. The training, created by LinkedIn Learning, was intended to address unconscious bias but was criticized as promoting racial stereotypes and creating hostile environments for white employees.

The incident demonstrates how DEI initiatives can become counterproductive when they rely on oversimplified identity categories or shame-based approaches. What was intended to promote inclusion was perceived by many as discriminatory and divisive.

Coca-Cola's response showed the challenge organizations face when diversity efforts generate controversy: defending the training risked appearing tone-deaf, while abandoning it risked appearing uncommitted to inclusion. The incident illustrates why implementation matters as much as intention in DEI work.

Case Study: Harvard's Affirmative Action Practices

Harvard's admissions practices illustrate how well-intentioned diversity efforts can create new forms of discrimination when they rely on racial quotas or subjective criteria that disadvantage certain groups. The university's consideration of race in admissions was challenged as discriminatory against Asian American applicants.

The case shows how diversity programs can become ethically problematic when they create different standards for different groups instead of removing barriers that prevent equal consideration. Harvard's "personality" ratings systematically disadvantaged Asian American applicants in ways that suggested bias instead of holistic evaluation.

The university's defense of its practices relied on arguments about diversity benefits that couldn't justify the methods used to achieve demographic targets. The disconnect between stated goals and practices undermined the ethical foundation of the program.

The Supreme Court's decision against race-conscious admissions shows how diversity efforts must evolve to focus on socioeconomic barriers and other factors that affect opportunity without relying on racial classifications.

Case Study: X's DEI rollback: when culture shifts fast

When Elon Musk acquired Twitter in 2022 and rebranded it X, the company eliminated its entire DEI team and associated programs almost immediately. The abrupt reversal of years of inclusion initiatives demonstrated how quickly organizational culture can shift when leadership changes — and what happens to employees caught in the transition.

Employees from underrepresented groups who had been recruited specifically under diversity initiatives found themselves at a company that had publicly abandoned the values that attracted them. Retention of these employees dropped sharply, illustrating that DEI isn't just about hiring numbers but about the sustained culture that makes people want to stay.

The case also showed how performative DEI — programs that exist primarily as public signals rather than genuine culture change — is fragile. When the business rationale shifted, the programs disappeared overnight because they had never been deeply embedded in how the organization actually operated. Organizations that treat DEI as a standalone initiative disconnected from core business culture will find it vulnerable to exactly this kind of wholesale reversal when leadership or priorities change.

Chapter 15: When the Company is Not Ethical

Working for an unethical company is like being a passenger on the Titanic after you've spotted the iceberg but before anyone else believes you. You can see the problems clearly, you know where things are heading, but you're trapped on a ship that's determined to stay its course. The question becomes whether you try to save the ship, save yourself, or find a way to warn others before impact.

Systemic organizational corruption runs deeper than individual bad actors or isolated incidents. When unethical behavior is woven into company culture, business models, or standard operating procedures, you're not dealing with people who've made poor choices; you're dealing with institutions that have built their success on practices that are fundamentally harmful to employees, customers, or society.

Business model corruption occurs when companies make money through practices that are inherently exploitative or harmful. The payday lending industry that profits from people's financial desperation, the social media platforms whose revenue depends on addiction and engagement regardless of psychological harm, or the pharmaceutical companies that price life-saving medications beyond reach while spending more on marketing than research.

These aren't companies that have ethical problems; these are companies whose entire reason for existence creates ethical problems. No amount of individual integrity or good intentions can fix business models that require harming people to generate profits.

Revenue stream ethics become impossible to ignore when you realize that every dollar of your salary comes from practices you find morally objectionable. The tobacco company that markets to teenagers in developing countries, the defense contractor that lobbies for unnecessary wars, or the tech company that sells surveillance tools to authoritarian governments all create situations where doing your job well means contributing to harm.

The scale of institutional wrongdoing differentiates corporate ethics violations from individual misconduct. When a single manager discriminates against employees, that's a management problem. When discrimination is built into hiring algorithms, performance evaluation systems, and promotion criteria across an entire organization, that's institutional racism affecting thousands of people.

Regulatory capture happens when the agencies supposed to oversee industries become controlled by the industries they're meant to regulate. The financial regulators staffed by former Wall Street executives, the environmental agencies led by former oil company lobbyists, or the healthcare regulators dominated by pharmaceutical industry veterans all create situations where systematic wrongdoing becomes legally protected.

When regulatory agencies are captured, traditional accountability mechanisms don't work. Companies can engage in harmful practices with impunity because the people responsible for stopping them are either former colleagues or future employers.

Cultural institutionalization of unethical practices creates environments where wrongdoing becomes so normalized that people stop recognizing it as problematic. The consulting firm where everyone inflates their hours, the advertising agency where everyone lies about campaign results, or the financial services company where everyone misleads clients about fees and risks.

These cultures create their own internal logic where participating in unethical behavior becomes a requirement for advancement and refusing to participate marks you as naive or uncommitted. The peer pressure to conform becomes overwhelming when everyone around you has already compromised their integrity.

Industry-wide ethical failures affect entire sectors where unethical practices have become standard operating procedures. The automotive industry's systematic emissions fraud, the banking sector's predatory lending practices, or the tech industry's privacy violations all represent cases where individual companies can't solve problems that require collective action and regulatory intervention.

When entire industries operate unethically, individual companies face competitive pressure to participate in harmful practices or lose market share to competitors who are willing to cut ethical corners. The race to the bottom becomes inevitable without external intervention.

Supply chain complicity extends corporate responsibility beyond direct operations to include the practices of vendors, suppliers, and business partners. The clothing retailer that sources from factories using child labor, the electronics manufacturer that buys minerals from conflict zones, or the food company that purchases from farms using exploitative labor practices all participate in harmful systems even when they don't directly engage in harmful activities.

Global operations create opportunities for ethical arbitrage where companies move harmful practices to jurisdictions with weaker regulations, lower labor standards, or less effective enforcement. The chemical company that dumps waste in developing countries, the tech firm that stores data in countries without privacy protections, or the manufacturer that relocates to avoid environmental regulations all exploit regulatory differences to engage in practices they couldn't pursue domestically.

Environmental externalities represent costs that companies impose on society without paying for them. The fossil fuel industry's contribution to climate change, the chemical industry's pollution of water supplies, or the agriculture industry's contribution to antibiotic resistance all create costs that are borne by society while profits are captured by shareholders.

When companies systematically externalize costs while privatizing benefits, they're essentially stealing from future generations and vulnerable populations who bear the consequences of decisions they didn't make and profits they don't share.

Financial engineering can obscure unethical practices through complex structures that make it difficult to understand what companies do or where their money comes from. The private equity firms that load companies with debt and extract fees while destroying jobs, the hedge funds that manipulate markets through high-frequency trading, or the cryptocurrency platforms that facilitate money laundering while claiming to democratize finance.

Stakeholder capitalism rhetoric often serves as cover for continued shareholder primacy in practice. Companies that issue sustainability reports while increasing their carbon footprints, that publish diversity statements while maintaining homogeneous leadership, or that promote worker welfare while fighting unionization efforts all engage in systematic hypocrisy that's worse than honest selfishness.

The scope of corporate influence extends beyond direct business operations to include lobbying, political donations, think tank funding, and media manipulation designed to shape public policy and opinion in favor of corporate interests regardless of public welfare.

When companies spend more money influencing policy than they do on research and development, when they fund climate denial despite internal research confirming climate change, or when they lobby against safety regulations while knowing their products cause harm, they're working against the public interest.

Institutional memory and culture perpetuation ensure that unethical practices survive changes in leadership, scandals, and public pressure. The banks that repeatedly engage in fraud despite massive fines, the pharmaceutical companies that continue deceptive marketing despite criminal convictions, or the tech platforms that persist in harmful practices despite congressional hearings all demonstrate how institutional corruption becomes self-perpetuating.

Corporate personhood legal fiction allows companies to claim rights while avoiding responsibilities, to pursue profits while externalizing costs, and to influence politics while avoiding accountability. When institutions designed to serve society become focused on extracting value from society, they create systematic conflicts between private gain and public welfare.

When the company is not ethical at the institutional level, individual responses are necessary but insufficient. Systematic problems require systematic solutions through regulation, enforcement, market pressure, and collective action that goes beyond what any individual employee can achieve.

The recognition that some organizations are fundamentally corrupt doesn't mean giving up on the possibility of ethical business practices, but it does mean understanding the difference between companies that can be reformed and companies that need to be replaced or heavily regulated.

Working for systematically unethical companies forces people to choose between their integrity and their livelihood, but pretending that individual virtue can solve institutional corruption is both naive and unfair to the people trapped in these systems.

Case Study: Facebook's Internal Research on Instagram: When Companies Know They're Causing Harm

Internal Facebook documents revealed that the company's own research showed Instagram was harmful to teenage mental health, among girls struggling with body image and self-esteem. Despite this knowledge, Facebook continued promoting Instagram to younger users and downplayed the mental health risks publicly.

The documents showed systematic corporate behavior where profit considerations outweighed user welfare. Employees raised concerns internally, but business priorities consistently won over safety considerations. The company had the research showing harm but chose to suppress instead of address it.

This case illustrates institutional corruption where individual employees might have good intentions, but systemic incentives ensure harmful outcomes. It shows how companies can become ethically compromised when their business models depend on outcomes they know are harmful to users.

Case Study: Patagonia's Activist Business Model

Patagonia's approach to corporate activism shows how companies can integrate social responsibility into their business model instead of treating it as separate from profit-making activities. The company's environmental activism is central to its brand and business strategy.

Founder Yvon Chouinard's decision to transfer ownership to environmental organizations demonstrates how business success can serve social goals instead of just private wealth accumulation. This approach aligns business incentives with social impact.

Patagonia's supply chain practices, product design decisions, and political advocacy all reflect environmental values that sometimes conflict with short-term profit maximization but support long-term sustainability and brand loyalty.

The company's success shows that ethical business practices can create competitive advantages when they're authentic and consistently applied instead of just marketing strategies.

Case Study: Philip Morris' Tobacco Marketing

Philip Morris' decades-long campaign to hide the health risks of smoking while marketing cigarettes to vulnerable populations represents systematic corporate wrongdoing that prioritized profits over public health.

The company's internal documents revealed that executives knew about smoking's health risks while publicly denying them and funding research designed to create doubt about scientific consensus. This deliberate deception continued for decades and affected millions of lives.

Philip Morris targeted marketing toward young people, low-income communities, and developing countries where regulation was weaker. These practices showed how companies can exploit vulnerable populations when profit motives override ethical constraints.

The eventual legal settlements and regulatory restrictions on tobacco marketing demonstrate how systematic corporate wrongdoing eventually faces consequences, but often only after causing enormous harm that could have been prevented.

Chapter 16: Case Study - Enron: When Everything Goes Wrong

Enron wasn't just a company that failed; it was a masterclass in how ethical rot can spread through an organization until nothing honest remains. What started as an energy trading company became a house of cards built on accounting fraud, executive greed, and a culture that rewarded deception over performance. The collapse destroyed not just Enron but entire industries that depended on financial transparency.

The seeds of Enron's destruction were planted in its culture, not its balance sheets. CEO Jeff Skilling created a "rank and yank" performance system that pitted employees against each other and rewarded short-term results regardless of how they were achieved. The bottom 10% of performers were fired annually, creating an environment where survival depended on making your numbers by any means necessary.

This performance culture was fundamentally unethical because it rewarded lying over truth-telling. Employees who raised concerns about questionable practices were marginalized or fired, while those who helped inflate revenues and hide losses were promoted. The system didn't just tolerate fraud; it required fraud to function.

Chairman Ken Lay and CFO Andy Fastow perfected the art of financial engineering, creating special purpose entities (SPEs) that moved debt off Enron's books while generating fake profits. These weren't clever accounting tricks; they were deliberate attempts to deceive investors, regulators, and employees about the company's true financial condition.

The ethical violations were systematic and pervasive. Executives sold their stock while encouraging employees to buy more. They reported profits that didn't exist while accumulating debt they didn't disclose. They created partnerships that enriched executives personally while bankrupting the company.

Every level of leadership was complicit in maintaining lies that everyone knew were unsustainable.

Enron's board of directors failed in their most basic ethical obligation: oversight. They approved suspicious transactions without adequate scrutiny, waived conflicts of interest policies when convenient, and collected fees for rubber-stamping management decisions. The board wasn't just incompetent; they were willfully blind to obvious problems.

The accounting firm Arthur Andersen destroyed its reputation and ultimately its existence by enabling Enron's fraud. Andersen auditors shredded documents, approved questionable accounting practices, and prioritized consulting fees over audit integrity. When your auditor becomes your accomplice, the entire system of financial transparency collapses.

Wall Street analysts and investment banks were complicit in maintaining the illusion of Enron's success. They issued buy recommendations while privately questioning the company's business model, helped structure the fraudulent partnerships, and collected millions in fees for enabling the deception. The financial industry's credibility was damaged because everyone was making money from the lie.

Individual employees faced impossible ethical choices in this environment. Speaking up about problems meant career suicide, but staying silent meant becoming complicit in fraud that was harming investors and fellow employees. Many people knew something was wrong but felt powerless to stop it without destroying their own livelihoods.

Sherron Watkins, an Enron vice president, became famous for her internal memo warning Ken Lay about accounting improprieties in August 2001. The collapse followed months later. Her memo wasn't early enough to force real change — by then the house of cards was already falling — and it wasn't late enough to save her career either. She exemplified the courage required to speak truth to power and the personal cost of ethical behavior in corrupt organizations.

The human cost of Enron's collapse was devastating. Employees lost their jobs, their pensions, and their faith in corporate America. Many had invested their retirement savings in Enron stock based on management's assurances, only to watch their life savings evaporate when the truth emerged. The personal betrayal was as damaging as the financial loss.

The regulatory response included the Sarbanes-Oxley Act, requiring CEOs and CFOs to personally certify their companies' financial statements. But legislation can't solve cultural problems or create integrity where none exists. The real lesson of Enron is that ethical behavior must be embedded in organizational DNA, not imposed through compliance programs.

Enron's collapse revealed how interconnected the financial system had become and how fraud in one company could damage entire industries. The accounting profession lost credibility, energy markets became suspect, and investor confidence was shattered. The ripple effects lasted for years and changed how business is conducted across multiple sectors.

The tragedy of Enron is that it was preventable. Multiple people at multiple organizations knew that something was fundamentally wrong, but institutional incentives discouraged honest reporting and rewarded willful blindness. The company failed not because of market forces or competitive pressures, but because ethical failures compounded until the entire structure collapsed.

Enron demonstrates what happens when short-term thinking completely overwhelms long-term sustainability. Every decision was made to maximize immediate returns regardless of future consequences. This approach works until it doesn't, and when it fails, the damage affects everyone who trusted the system to operate honestly.

The case shows how individual ethical failures can become institutional corruption when they're systematically rewarded and embedded in company culture. Enron wasn't brought down by one bad actor but by a culture that made bad actors inevitable and honest actors unemployable.

Most importantly, Enron proves that ethical business practices aren't just moral imperatives; they're practical necessities. Companies that operate through deception and fraud will eventually collapse, taking down everyone associated with them. The short-term gains from unethical behavior are always overwhelmed by the long-term costs of systematic dishonesty.

Chapter 17: Case Study - Theranos: The Charismatic Leader's Deception

Elizabeth Holmes didn't just run a fraudulent company; she created a cult of personality so powerful that brilliant people convinced themselves that obvious lies were revolutionary truths. Theranos represents the dark side of Silicon Valley's "fake it till you make it" culture, where charismatic leadership and compelling narratives can override scientific reality and ethical judgment for surprisingly long periods.

Holmes' genius wasn't in technology; it was in manipulation. She understood that people want to believe in revolutionary breakthroughs and charismatic leaders, especially when those breakthroughs promise to save lives and disrupt established industries. She crafted a narrative so compelling that investors, board members, and employees suspended their critical thinking to participate in what they thought was history in the making.

The fundamental ethical violation at Theranos was lying about the core technology. Holmes claimed that her "Edison" machines could run hundreds of tests on a single drop of blood, but the machines never worked as advertised. Most tests were run on traditional machines using conventional blood draws, while results were manipulated to hide the technology's failures.

This wasn't a case of overpromising about future capabilities; it was deliberate deception about current reality. Patients received inaccurate test results that could have affected their medical treatment. Investors committed hundreds of millions of dollars based on demonstrations that were entirely fake. The lie wasn't about potential; it was about present-day functionality.

Holmes' board of directors reads like a who's who of American establishment figures: former Secretaries of State, Defense, and Treasury, along with prominent business leaders and politicians. But none of them had relevant medical or scientific expertise, and they served primarily as window dressing to legitimize the company instead of providing meaningful oversight.

The board's composition was ethically problematic because it prioritized prestige over competence. Board members were chosen for their reputations and connections instead of their ability to evaluate the company's technology or business model. This created a governance structure designed to impress outsiders instead of protect stakeholders.

Ramesh "Sunny" Balwani, Holmes' business partner and romantic partner, exemplified the toxic management culture that pervaded Theranos. He used intimidation, secrecy, and paranoia to suppress dissent and maintain the illusion of progress. Employees who asked questions or raised concerns were fired, demoted, or marginalized.

The management approach was ethically bankrupt because it prioritized maintaining deception over solving problems. Instead of addressing technology failures, management focused on silencing people who pointed out those failures. The company's energy went into covering up problems instead of fixing them.

Theranos attracted talented scientists and engineers who genuinely believed they were working on revolutionary technology that would improve healthcare. Many discovered that the technology didn't work as advertised but were trapped by legal agreements, financial needs, or fear of retaliation. The company exploited people's good intentions and professional aspirations.

The ethical dilemma for employees was stark: continue working for a company they knew was deceptive, or risk their careers by speaking out against a powerful and litigious organization. Many chose to leave quietly instead of blow the whistle, allowing the deception to continue while protecting themselves from legal and professional retaliation.

Tyler Shultz, grandson of board member George Shultz (the former Secretary of State who died in 2021), and Erika Cheung became the most prominent whistleblowers, ultimately speaking to regulators and journalists about the company's fraudulent practices. Their courage in speaking out despite personal and professional risks exemplifies ethical behavior in impossible circumstances.

The personal cost of whistleblowing was severe. Both faced legal threats, financial pressure, and family conflicts. Tyler Shultz's relationship with his grandfather was severely strained — George Shultz initially defended Holmes and Theranos against his grandson's allegations, a conflict that persisted for years before his death in 2021. The whistleblowers' experience shows how ethical behavior can exact profound personal costs.

John Carreyrou's investigative reporting for the Wall Street Journal was crucial in exposing Theranos' fraud, but he faced intense legal and personal pressure from the company. Holmes and her legal team used intimidation tactics to try to prevent publication of stories that would reveal the truth about the technology.

The media's role in the Theranos saga was complex. Many outlets initially celebrated Holmes as a visionary entrepreneur without adequately investigating her claims. The business press's tendency to promote compelling narratives over rigorous fact-checking enabled the fraud to continue longer than it should have.

Investor due diligence failures were endemic throughout the Theranos saga. Major investors committed hundreds of millions of dollars without adequately verifying the company's technological claims or requiring independent validation of test results. The allure of revolutionary technology and charismatic leadership overcame basic investment discipline.

The regulatory response was slow and inadequate. The FDA and other agencies had authority to investigate Theranos' claims but didn't act decisively until journalists and whistleblowers forced their hand. The failure of regulatory oversight allowed fraudulent medical testing to continue for years.

Patient harm was the most serious consequence of Theranos' fraud. People received inaccurate test results that could have led to inappropriate medical decisions, unnecessary anxiety, or delayed treatment for serious conditions. The company's deception put real people's health at risk for the sake of maintaining investment funding.

The criminal prosecution of Holmes and Balwani established important precedents about holding executives accountable for corporate fraud. Holmes' conviction on fraud charges relating to investors (but not patients) sent a message about the consequences of deceiving stakeholders, even when wrapped in compelling narratives about technological innovation.

Theranos demonstrates how charismatic leadership can become a dangerous substitute for competence and honesty. Holmes' ability to inspire confidence and attract support allowed her to build a billion-dollar company based on technology that didn't work and claims that weren't true.

The case shows how Silicon Valley's culture of disruption and rapid growth can enable fraud when enthusiasm for innovation overwhelms skeptical evaluation of capabilities. The pressure to achieve breakthrough results can lead to cutting corners that ultimately undermine the very innovation the culture is supposed to promote.

Most importantly, Theranos proves that good intentions don't justify bad methods. Even if Holmes genuinely believed her technology would eventually work, the deception about current capabilities was unethical and harmful. The ends don't justify the means when the means involve systematic lying to patients, investors, and employees.

Chapter 18: Case Study - Wells Fargo: Pressure, Incentives, and Individual Choice

Wells Fargo's fake account scandal reveals how organizational pressure and perverse incentives can turn ordinary employees into unwitting participants in systematic fraud. Unlike Enron's executive-driven corruption or Theranos' technological deception, Wells Fargo's problems emerged from the ground up when impossible sales goals made ethical behavior incompatible with job survival.

The scandal began with aggressive sales goals that required employees to sell multiple financial products to every customer, regardless of whether those products served the customer's needs. Branch employees were expected to achieve "Eight is Great" - selling eight different products to each customer - even though most customers needed only basic banking services.

These sales targets weren't just ambitious; they were deliberately impossible to achieve through legitimate means. Wells Fargo executives set goals they knew required deceptive practices, then claimed ignorance when employees did whatever was necessary to meet those expectations. The company created systematic pressure to commit fraud while maintaining plausible deniability about the results.

Front-line employees faced an impossible ethical choice: meet unrealistic sales goals through fraudulent means or lose their jobs for failing to perform. Many chose to open unauthorized accounts, apply for unwanted credit cards, and enroll customers in services they didn't request. The fraud wasn't motivated by personal greed but by survival in a toxic work environment.

The human cost was severe for both employees and customers. Workers suffered stress, anxiety, and moral injury from being forced to deceive customers daily. Many quit or were fired for refusing to participate in fraudulent practices. Customers discovered unauthorized accounts on their credit reports, were charged fees for services they didn't use, and lost trust in an institution they had relied on for decades.

Branch managers were caught in the middle, pressuring employees to meet impossible goals while being pressured by their own supervisors to deliver results. Many knew that the sales practices were fraudulent but felt powerless to change a system that rewarded fraud and punished honesty. The toxic culture flowed from the top down through every level of management.

The incentive structure was fundamentally corrupted because it rewarded behavior that harmed customers and the bank's long-term interests. Employees who met sales goals through fraud were promoted and celebrated, while those who tried to serve customers honestly were marginalized or fired. The system made bad actors successful and good actors unemployable.

Senior executives, CEO John Stumpf and retail banking head Carrie Tolstedt, claimed they were unaware of the systematic fraud occurring throughout their organization. This willful blindness was ethically indefensible given the scope and duration of the problems. Leaders who create pressure systems that require fraud can't claim innocence when fraud occurs.

The board of directors failed in their oversight responsibilities by not questioning how the bank was achieving such impressive cross-selling results. The "Eight is Great" strategy should have raised red flags about whether customer needs were driving sales or whether employees were being pressured to sell unnecessary products.

Wells Fargo's corporate culture prioritized short-term sales metrics over long-term customer relationships and institutional integrity. The bank's emphasis on quarterly earnings and growth targets created pressure throughout the organization to achieve results regardless of methods. This culture made the fake account scandal inevitable instead of accidental.

The regulatory response was swift but arguably insufficient. Wells Fargo paid billions in fines and faced regulatory restrictions on its growth, but the individual executives who created the toxic culture faced relatively minor consequences. The disconnect between institutional penalties and individual accountability sent mixed messages about responsibility for corporate wrongdoing.

Employee whistleblowing was met with retaliation instead of investigation. Workers who reported fraudulent practices to management, ethics hotlines, or regulators faced discipline, termination, or hostile work environments. The bank's response to internal complaints demonstrated that leadership was more interested in suppressing information about problems than solving them.

The scandal's scope was staggering: over 3.5 million unauthorized accounts were opened over several years, affecting millions of customers and thousands of employees. The systematic nature of the fraud showed that it wasn't the result of a few bad actors but of institutional pressure that made fraudulent behavior necessary for employment survival.

Congressional hearings exposed the disconnect between executive compensation and accountability. While front-line employees were fired for following the incentives their leaders created, executives like Tolstedt retired with multimillion-dollar packages despite overseeing systematic fraud. The disparity in consequences reflected broader problems with corporate accountability.

The fake account scandal damaged Wells Fargo's reputation and customer relationships in ways that took years to repair. Customer trust, once lost, is difficult to rebuild, and the bank faced ongoing scrutiny from regulators, customers, and employees. The short-term gains from aggressive sales tactics were overwhelmed by the long-term costs of systematic deception.

The case demonstrates how organizational design can make ethical behavior practically impossible. When companies create systems that require employees to choose between their integrity and their livelihoods, many will choose survival. The responsibility lies with leaders who design these systems, not just with employees who navigate them.

Wells Fargo's experience shows how performance metrics can become corrupted when they're disconnected from genuine value creation. Measuring success through cross-selling numbers instead of customer satisfaction or long-term relationship quality created incentives that ultimately harmed both customers and the institution.

The scandal illustrates the danger of setting goals without considering how they'll be achieved. Leaders who demand results without providing ethical means to achieve them bear responsibility for the unethical methods that employees inevitably adopt. Good intentions about growth and performance don't excuse willful blindness about implementation.

Most importantly, Wells Fargo proves that ethical problems compound when they're ignored or suppressed. The bank had numerous opportunities to address the fraudulent sales practices before they became a national scandal, but leadership chose to maintain the profitable system instead of confront its ethical problems.

The case serves as a warning about how ordinary people can become complicit in systematic wrongdoing when organizational pressures override individual moral judgment. Creating ethical workplaces requires designing systems that make honest behavior practical and sustainable, not just expected.

Chapter 19: Case Study - Cambridge Analytica/Facebook: Data Ethics in Action

The Cambridge Analytica scandal represents a perfect storm of data ethics violations that exposed how personal information harvested from social media could be weaponized for political manipulation. The case reveals the ethical complexities of data ownership, consent, and responsibility in the digital age, while demonstrating how Facebook's "move fast and break things" culture enabled systematic privacy violations.

Cambridge Analytica obtained personal data from millions of Facebook users through a personality quiz app created by researcher Aleksandr Kogan, who operated through his own company, Global Science Research. The app harvested data not just from people who took the quiz but from their Facebook friends as well. Kogan then shared that data with Cambridge Analytica — in violation of his agreement with Facebook — giving the political consultancy access to detailed profiles of tens of millions of users who had never interacted with the app at all.

The ethical violation began with deceptive data collection. Users who took the personality quiz thought they were contributing to academic research, not providing personal information for political campaigns. The app's terms buried the true purpose of data collection in dense legal language that most users didn't read or understand. Consent obtained through deception isn't meaningful consent.

Facebook's platform design enabled this massive data harvesting because the company prioritized developer access and user engagement over privacy protection. The social network's APIs allowed third-party apps to access not just the data of users who installed them, but also information about those users' friends. This design choice put profits before privacy rights.

The scope of the data collection was staggering: information from over 87 million Facebook users was harvested without their knowledge or consent. This included personal details, political preferences, psychological profiles, and social connections that could be used to create detailed portraits of individual users' personalities and vulnerabilities.

Cambridge Analytica used this data to create psychological profiles for political targeting during the 2016 U.S. presidential election and Brexit referendum. The company claimed it could identify personality traits that made people susceptible to certain political messages and then micro-target them with customized propaganda designed to influence their voting behavior.

The political manipulation aspect raised fundamental questions about democratic processes and informed consent in political discourse. If voters are being targeted with personalized propaganda based on their psychological vulnerabilities, can they make truly informed political choices? The case exposed how data analytics could undermine democratic deliberation.

Steve Bannon and Robert Mercer, key figures in conservative politics, funded Cambridge Analytica's work and used the harvested data to support Donald Trump's presidential campaign. This connection between data harvesting and political outcomes demonstrated how privacy violations could have real-world consequences for democratic processes and political representation.

Facebook's initial response to reports about Cambridge Analytica was inadequate and deceptive. The company downplayed the scope of the data harvesting, characterized it as a "breach" instead of a feature of their platform design, and failed to notify affected users promptly. This response showed how the company prioritized reputation management over accountability and user protection.

Mark Zuckerberg's congressional testimony revealed the extent to which Facebook's leadership didn't understand or take responsibility for their platform's impact on privacy and democracy. Zuckerberg's evasive answers and claims of ignorance about basic platform functions demonstrated that the company's growth had outpaced its ethical development.

The role of whistleblower Christopher Wylie was crucial in exposing the scandal. Wylie, a former Cambridge Analytica employee, revealed the data harvesting operation and its political applications to journalists and regulators. His decision to speak out despite personal and legal risks exemplified the importance of insider accountability in complex technological systems.

Journalist Carole Cadwalladr's reporting for The Guardian was essential in bringing the Cambridge Analytica story to public attention. Her investigative work showed how data harvesting connected to political manipulation and democratic interference. The case demonstrated the critical role of journalism in holding technology companies accountable for their societal impact.

The regulatory response was global and significant. Facebook faced investigations and fines from regulators in multiple countries, including a $5 billion penalty from the Federal Trade Commission. The scandal accelerated discussions about data protection regulations like the European Union's General Data Protection Regulation (GDPR).

Employee reactions within Facebook were mixed, with some workers expressing concern about the company's privacy practices while others defended the platform's role in connecting people and enabling free expression. The internal debate reflected broader tensions between technological innovation and social responsibility.

The scandal damaged Facebook's reputation and user trust, leading to congressional hearings, regulatory investigations, and public campaigns encouraging users to delete their accounts. The company faced sustained criticism about its business model, which depends on collecting and monetizing personal data for advertising purposes.

Cambridge Analytica's closure following the scandal showed how data misuse could destroy companies even when the underlying practices were widespread in the industry. The company became a symbol of data exploitation and political manipulation, making its brand toxic to clients and partners.

The case exposed fundamental problems with the informed consent model for data collection. Users can't meaningfully consent to data uses they don't understand, and terms of service agreements are too complex for most people to comprehend. The traditional model of privacy protection through individual consent is inadequate for complex data ecosystems.

Facebook's business model creates inherent conflicts between user privacy and corporate profits. The company makes money by collecting personal data and selling access to users' attention through targeted advertising. This model incentivizes maximizing data collection and user engagement instead of protecting privacy and promoting healthy social interactions.

The Cambridge Analytica scandal demonstrates how individual privacy violations can aggregate into threats to democratic institutions and social cohesion. When personal data is used to manipulate political behavior, privacy becomes not just an individual right but a collective necessity for democratic governance.

The case illustrates the global nature of data ethics challenges. Information collected in one country can be processed in another and used to influence political processes in a third. Traditional regulatory approaches based on national sovereignty are inadequate for addressing the cross-border nature of digital platforms and data flows.

Most importantly, Cambridge Analytica shows how technological capabilities can outpace ethical frameworks and regulatory systems. The ability to collect, analyze, and act on personal data at massive scale developed faster than society's ability to understand and govern these capabilities. The scandal serves as a warning about the need for proactive instead of reactive approaches to technology governance.

Chapter 20: Case Study - Microsoft: Getting Ethics Right

Microsoft's transformation under CEO Satya Nadella provides a compelling example of how organizations can rebuild their culture around ethical principles without sacrificing business performance. The company's journey from a combative, winner-take-all culture to one focused on empowerment and inclusion demonstrates that ethical business practices can be a competitive advantage instead of a constraint.

When Nadella became CEO in 2014, Microsoft was struggling with a reputation for aggressive business practices, internal competition, and a culture that many described as toxic. The company's "stack ranking" performance system pitted employees against each other, creating an environment where collaboration was discouraged and individual achievement was prioritized over team success.

Nadella's first major change was eliminating the stack ranking system and replacing it with a culture focused on growth mindset, collaboration, and learning from failure. This shift required fundamentally changing how the company evaluated performance, rewarded success, and responded to mistakes. The new approach emphasized continuous improvement over zero-sum competition.

The culture change wasn't just about internal dynamics; it extended to how Microsoft engaged with competitors and partners. Under previous leadership, the company was known for aggressive tactics against competitors and attempts to control entire technology markets. Nadella shifted toward collaboration, open-source development, and platform strategies that benefited multiple stakeholders. The new culture faced a concrete test in 2018 when employees organized over a US Army contract to supply HoloLens technology for combat use. Workers argued it conflicted with the values Microsoft had been building. Leadership didn't cancel the contract, but they engaged directly with concerned employees, created transfer options for those who objected, and published clearer guidelines on military contracts going forward. Whether or not the ultimate decision was right, the episode revealed something real: Nadella's culture had produced employees confident enough to push back and a leadership team that engaged rather than suppressed.

Microsoft's approach to artificial intelligence demonstrates how the company has embedded ethical considerations into product development. The company established AI ethics principles focusing on fairness, accountability, transparency, and human oversight. These aren't just marketing statements; they're integrated into the development process through ethics reviews and algorithmic testing.

The company's AI for Good initiative represents a commitment to using technology for social benefit instead of just profit maximization. Microsoft has committed significant resources to projects addressing climate change, accessibility, humanitarian crises, and cultural preservation. This approach shows how business success can align with social responsibility.

Diversity and inclusion efforts at Microsoft go beyond typical corporate programs to address systemic barriers and create genuine culture change. The company has tied executive compensation to diversity metrics, increased representation in leadership positions, and created inclusive design practices that consider diverse user needs from the beginning of product development.

The company's response to employee activism shows how organizations can maintain ethical cultures while managing diverse viewpoints. When employees raised concerns about government contracts and immigration policies, Microsoft leadership engaged in dialogue, made policy changes, and allowed employees to transfer away from projects they found objectionable without career penalties.

Microsoft's privacy and security practices demonstrate how companies can balance business interests with user protection. The company has adopted strong encryption, limited data collection, and transparent reporting about government requests for user information. These practices sometimes conflict with short-term revenue opportunities but support long-term trust and user loyalty.

The company's approach to accessibility illustrates how ethical considerations can drive innovation that benefits everyone. Microsoft's investment in accessibility features for people with disabilities has led to products and services that improve usability for all users while creating new market opportunities and demonstrating social responsibility.

Environmental sustainability initiatives at Microsoft show how companies can address climate change while maintaining growth and profitability. The company has committed to being carbon negative by 2030 and removing all historical carbon emissions by 2050. These goals require fundamental changes to operations, supply chains, and product design.

Microsoft's handling of the SolarWinds cyberattack response demonstrated responsible disclosure practices and collaboration with government agencies and security researchers. Instead of minimizing the incident or deflecting responsibility, the company provided transparent information and worked collaboratively to address the security vulnerability.

The company's approach to platform responsibility on LinkedIn shows how social media companies can moderate content while respecting free expression. Microsoft has invested in AI-powered tools to detect harassment and misinformation while maintaining policies that allow diverse viewpoints and robust debate within professional contexts.

Employee wellbeing initiatives at Microsoft address the mental health and work-life integration challenges that affect many technology workers. The company has expanded mental health benefits, implemented flexible work arrangements, and created programs to prevent burnout and support employee development throughout their careers.

Microsoft's supply chain ethics demonstrate how large corporations can extend their values throughout their business relationships. The company requires suppliers to meet labor standards, environmental requirements, and human rights commitments. These standards sometimes increase costs but ensure that business success doesn't depend on exploitation.

The company's approach to emerging technologies like quantum computing and mixed reality shows how organizations can consider ethical implications early in the development process instead of addressing them after problems emerge. Microsoft has engaged with ethicists, policymakers, and civil society organizations to anticipate challenges and build safeguards into new technologies.

Leadership development at Microsoft emphasizes ethical decision-making and inclusive leadership as core competencies. The company trains managers to recognize bias, navigate ethical dilemmas, and create psychologically safe environments where employees can raise concerns without fear of retaliation.

Microsoft's transformation demonstrates that ethical business practices can improve financial performance instead of constraining it. The company's market value and employee satisfaction have increased significantly since implementing culture changes focused on ethical leadership and social responsibility.

The company's approach to government relations shows how corporations can engage with policy makers while maintaining independence and ethical standards. Microsoft advocates for responsible technology policies, supports democratic institutions, and provides technical expertise to policy makers without compromising its values or business integrity.

Corporate governance at Microsoft reflects the company's commitment to ethical leadership through board diversity, executive accountability, and transparent reporting. The company has implemented policies that align executive compensation with long-term value creation and stakeholder interests instead of just short-term financial metrics.

Microsoft's success in transforming its culture while maintaining business growth provides a roadmap for other organizations seeking to embed ethical practices throughout their operations. The company shows that ethical leadership isn't just about avoiding problems; it's about creating sustainable competitive advantages through trust, innovation, and stakeholder alignment.

Most importantly, Microsoft's experience demonstrates that cultural transformation is possible but requires sustained commitment from leadership, alignment between values and systems, and willingness to make short-term sacrifices for long-term benefits. The company's journey from ethical laggard to industry leader shows that organizations can change their fundamental character with the right leadership and commitment to ethical principles.

Chapter 21: Your Responsibility (Yes, Yours)

After twenty chapters of analyzing what everyone else is doing wrong, it's time for the uncomfortable part: what are you supposed to do about it? This isn't a question about what you should do in some theoretical perfect world where good behavior is always rewarded and bad behavior is always punished. This is about what you can do in the messy, complicated, often unfair world where you have to pay your bills and advance your career.

The first thing to understand is that you're not responsible for fixing every ethical problem you encounter. You're not Batman, and your workplace isn't Gotham City. Trying to single-handedly reform toxic cultures or take down corrupt executives is a good way to destroy your career without solving any problems. Your responsibility is more limited and more achievable: don't make things worse, and when possible, make them a little better.

This distinction matters because a lot of people get paralyzed by the scope of workplace ethical problems or burned out trying to solve everything at once. The goal isn't moral perfection; it's moral consistency within the constraints of your situation. You can't eliminate all workplace toxicity, but you can refuse to participate in creating it.

Your first responsibility is to yourself and your family. This isn't selfishness; it's recognizing that you can't help anyone else if you've destroyed your own career or financial security through reckless moral crusading. The people who depend on you deserve consideration in your ethical calculations. Sometimes the most responsible thing you can do is protect your ability to provide for them while looking for better opportunities.

But self-preservation isn't a blank check to ignore ethical problems or participate in harmful behavior. There's a difference between protecting yourself from retaliation and contributing to the problems you claim to oppose. You can choose not to blow the whistle on your boss's expense account fraud without helping them create fake receipts.

The responsibility starts with your own behavior. Are you honest in your communications? Do you take credit for other people's work? Do you keep your commitments? Do you treat colleagues fairly regardless of their usefulness to you? These aren't dramatic ethical dilemmas; they're daily choices that either contribute to or detract from workplace trust and functionality.

If you're in a management position, your responsibilities expand because your behavior affects other people's careers and wellbeing. The power to hire, fire, promote, and assign work comes with obligations that don't apply to individual contributors. You're responsible not just for your own choices but for the environment you create for the people who report to you.

Managers who claim they're "just following orders" or "don't have any choice" about how they treat their teams are usually lying to themselves and everyone else. You might not control overall company strategy, but you control how you communicate with your team, how you distribute work and recognition, and how you respond when people raise concerns. Those choices matter enormously to the people affected by them.

The "I didn't know" defense is hollow for managers because your job includes knowing what's happening in your organization. Willful ignorance isn't an ethical position; it's a failure of leadership. If you don't want to know about problems because knowing would require you to act, then you're part of the problem.

Senior leaders bear even greater responsibility because their decisions affect entire organizations and all the stakeholders connected to them. The CEO who claims they "had no idea" about systematic fraud occurring throughout their company is either incompetent or lying. The board member who rubber-stamps management decisions without asking hard questions is failing in their fiduciary duties.

But responsibility isn't just about the people at the top. Everyone has some sphere of influence, even if it's just their immediate colleagues or their own reputation. You're responsible for how you use whatever influence you have, whether it's mentoring junior employees, speaking up in meetings, or just modeling the behavior you want to see from others.

The bystander problem is real and pervasive in workplace settings. When you witness discrimination, harassment, fraud, or other harmful behavior, you have choices about how to respond. You don't have to become a whistleblower or confront powerful people directly, but you do have to decide whether you're going to be complicit through your silence.

Sometimes the most you can do is document what you've witnessed, support affected colleagues, or refuse to participate in questionable activities. These responses might seem inadequate, but they're better than pretending nothing happened or helping to cover up problems.

The documentation responsibility is important because institutional memory is often deliberately destroyed when problems become public. Your records might be the only evidence that certain events occurred or that people raised concerns before disasters happened. You're not required to become an investigative journalist, but keeping accurate records of problematic behavior serves both your interests and broader accountability.

Alliances with ethical colleagues help create environments where good behavior is supported instead of isolated. This doesn't mean organizing some kind of workplace resistance movement; it means identifying people who share your values and finding ways to support each other professionally. Ethical behavior is easier when you're not doing it alone.

The responsibility extends to your choice of employers and career decisions. While you can't always control every aspect of your work situation, you do have some choice about what organizations you join and what roles you pursue. Consistently choosing employers or positions that require you to compromise your integrity suggests that you value money or status more than ethical behavior.

This doesn't mean you have to work for nonprofits or turn down every job that involves moral complexity. But it does mean paying attention to organizational culture during the interview process, asking questions about how decisions are made and how problems are addressed, and being honest with yourself about what kinds of compromises you're willing to make.

Industry responsibility matters too, especially in sectors with social impact. If you work in finance, healthcare, technology, education, or other fields that affect public welfare, you bear some responsibility for how your industry operates. This might mean participating in professional organizations, supporting appropriate regulation, or speaking out when industry practices cause harm.

The consumer responsibility is often overlooked but increasingly important. The products you buy, the services you use, and the companies you invest in all reflect your values and influence corporate behavior through market mechanisms. You can't research every purchase decision, but you can pay attention to major ethical issues in industries where you spend money.

Political responsibility includes understanding how policy affects workplace ethics and supporting candidates and positions that promote fair labor practices, appropriate regulation, and accountability for corporate wrongdoing. Business ethics aren't separate from political choices; they're shaped by the legal and regulatory environment that political decisions create.

The responsibility for continuous learning means staying informed about ethical challenges in your field, understanding evolving best practices, and developing better judgment through experience and reflection. Ethical decision-making is a skill that improves with practice and deteriorates without it.

Teaching responsibility applies to anyone with more experience or knowledge than their colleagues. Sharing what you've learned about navigating ethical challenges, warning people about problematic situations, and modeling good behavior all contribute to better workplace cultures. You don't have to be perfect to help others avoid mistakes you've made.

The long-term perspective responsibility means considering how current decisions will affect your future options and reputation. The shortcuts you take today might limit your opportunities tomorrow. The relationships you damage through unethical behavior might be impossible to repair when you need them later. Ethical behavior is ultimately an investment in your long-term interests.

Your responsibility also includes accepting the consequences of your choices instead of blaming others when things don't work out as hoped. If you choose to stay in a toxic workplace for financial reasons, own that choice instead of claiming you had no alternatives. If you choose to speak up about problems and face retaliation, accept that risk as the price of maintaining your integrity.

The mentoring responsibility extends to helping junior colleagues understand workplace dynamics and ethical challenges they'll face. This doesn't mean lecturing people or imposing your values on them, but it does mean sharing practical wisdom about how to navigate difficult situations while maintaining professional integrity.

Personal responsibility includes managing your own stress, maintaining perspective, and taking care of your mental and physical health so that you can make good decisions under pressure. Ethical decision-making becomes much harder when you're overwhelmed, exhausted, or operating from a position of desperation.

The boundary-setting responsibility means being clear about what you will and won't do, communicating those boundaries appropriately, and maintaining them consistently even when it's inconvenient. People who don't know your limits will keep pushing until they find them.

Finally, your responsibility includes recognizing that workplace ethics aren't just about following rules or avoiding problems. They're about contributing to environments where people can do meaningful work, develop their capabilities, and contribute to organizations that create value instead of extract it.

You don't have to save the world, reform your industry, or become a perfect person. You just have to take responsibility for your own choices and their consequences. In a world full of people who claim they had no choice or didn't understand the implications of their actions, that's a pretty radical position.

The good news is that ethical behavior gets easier with practice. The more consistently you make decisions based on your values instead of just immediate self-interest, the more natural it becomes. The bad news is that you'll never stop facing situations where doing the right thing costs you something you want.

Your responsibility is to decide what kind of person you want to be professionally and then live consistently with that decision, even when it's inconvenient. Everything else is just details.

Conclusion

If you've made it this far, you either have an unusual tolerance for workplace ethics discussions or you're procrastinating on something more important. Either way, congratulations on making it through the moral minefield that is modern professional life.

The unfortunate truth is that ethical challenges in the workplace are getting more complex, not simpler. Technology is evolving faster than our ability to understand its implications. Work arrangements are changing faster than policies can adapt. Social expectations are shifting faster than organizational cultures can evolve. The old rules don't quite fit the new situations, and the new rules haven't been written yet.

This isn't an argument for giving up on ethics or accepting that "everyone does it" as a justification for cutting corners. It's recognition that navigating workplace ethics requires more thoughtful consideration than following a simple set of rules or compliance training modules. The scenarios you'll face will be messier, more ambiguous, and more consequential than the textbook examples.

The cases we've examined - from Enron's systematic corruption to Microsoft's cultural transformation - show that ethical behavior isn't just about individual virtue. It's about systems, incentives, leadership, and culture. Good people can make bad choices when they're trapped in toxic systems. Bad people can be constrained by good systems. Most importantly, organizational ethics aren't fixed; they can be changed through deliberate effort and sustained commitment.

The framework that emerges from these cases is surprisingly straightforward, even if the implementation is complex. Ethical workplaces require three things: clarity about values and expectations, systems that reward ethical behavior and punish unethical behavior, and leadership that models the standards they expect from others.

Clarity means more than mission statements and codes of conduct, though those help. It means honest conversations about trade-offs, transparent decision-making processes, and acknowledgment that ethical dilemmas don't always have perfect solutions. People can handle complexity and ambiguity, but they can't navigate ethical challenges when they don't understand what's expected.

Systems matter because individual virtue isn't scalable. When organizations rely solely on people's moral character to prevent problems, they're setting themselves up for failure. The right systems make ethical behavior practical and sustainable. The wrong systems make ethical behavior impossible, regardless of how good people's intentions might be.

Leadership accountability is crucial because culture flows from the top. When leaders say one thing and do another, everyone notices. When leaders create pressure that requires unethical behavior to meet targets, they bear responsibility for the results. When leaders protect their friends and punish truth-tellers, they're telling everyone what really matters.

The individual responsibility part is equally important. You can't control your organization's culture, but you can control your response to it. You can't eliminate all ethical dilemmas from your career, but you can develop the judgment to navigate them thoughtfully. You can't guarantee that doing the right thing will always work out perfectly, but you can ensure that you'll be able to live with your choices.

The practical advice that emerges from these cases is less inspiring than motivational posters but more useful than abstract principles. Document problematic behavior not because you're planning to become a whistleblower, but because accurate records help you understand patterns and protect yourself if situations escalate. Build relationships across your organization not because networking is fun, but because isolation makes you vulnerable to manipulation and limits your options when problems arise.

Develop financial independence not because money is everything, but because economic security gives you the freedom to make ethical choices even when they're costly. Build skills that are transferable across organizations not because loyalty is dead, but because the ability to leave gives you power to resist pressure to compromise your integrity.

Pay attention to early warning signs not because you're paranoid, but because small ethical compromises tend to compound into larger problems. Trust your instincts when something feels wrong not because your feelings are infallible, but because discomfort often signals ethical conflicts that your conscious mind hasn't fully processed yet.

The technology challenges we've discussed - artificial intelligence, data privacy, remote work, gig economy platforms - will continue evolving in ways we can't predict. But the underlying ethical principles remain constant: treat people fairly, be honest about capabilities and limitations, respect others' autonomy and dignity, and consider the broader consequences of your actions.

The diversity and inclusion challenges will also continue evolving as society's understanding of equity and fairness develops. But the core challenge remains building organizations where everyone can contribute their best work regardless of their background, where different perspectives are valued instead of just tolerated, and where inclusion is genuine instead of performative.

The leadership challenges aren't going away either. Power still corrupts, incentives still matter, and charismatic leaders can still lead organizations astray when their personal interests diverge from stakeholder welfare. But awareness of these patterns helps people recognize problems earlier and respond more effectively.

The most important insight from studying workplace ethics isn't that there are right answers to every dilemma, but that there are better and worse ways to approach difficult decisions. Better approaches involve seeking diverse perspectives, considering long-term consequences, acknowledging uncertainty and limitations, and prioritizing stakeholder welfare over personal advantage.

Better approaches also involve recognizing that ethical behavior isn't always rewarded immediately or obviously. Sometimes doing the right thing costs you opportunities, relationships, or financial benefits. But the alternative - compromising your integrity for short-term gains - typically costs more in the long run.

The goal isn't moral perfection, but moral progress. Organizations can become more ethical through deliberate effort. People can develop better ethical judgment through practice and reflection. Industries can establish better standards through collective action and regulatory pressure.

This progress happens through the accumulation of small decisions and incremental improvements instead of dramatic transformations. Most ethical progress is boring: better policies, clearer communication, more consistent enforcement, fairer systems. It's not inspiring, but it's effective.

The next time you face an ethical dilemma at work - and you will - remember that you're not the first person to encounter these challenges and you won't be the last. The details of your situation will be unique, but the underlying dynamics are familiar. Use the experiences of others to inform your thinking, but make your own decisions based on your values and circumstances.

Trust your judgment while remaining open to new information. Seek advice while accepting responsibility for your choices. Consider the consequences for yourself while also thinking about impacts on others. Balance idealism with pragmatism, but don't use pragmatism as an excuse for compromising your core principles.

Most importantly, remember that workplace ethics aren't just about avoiding problems or following rules. They're about creating environments where people can do meaningful work, build productive relationships, and contribute to organizations that make the world better instead of worse.

The workplace is where most of us spend most of our waking hours. It's where we develop skills, build relationships, and create value for ourselves and others. Making that environment more ethical isn't just a professional obligation; it's an investment in the kind of society we want to live in.

If this book has convinced you that workplace ethics matter and given you some tools for navigating the challenges you'll face, then it's accomplished its purpose. The rest is up to you. Try not to screw it up.

Books by Richard Lowe

See books by Richard Lowe at

https://masterofworlds.com

Get free publishing insights and industry updates at

https://thewritingking.substack.com

For ghostwriting and book coaching services see

https://thewritingking.com